D1076237

Editior

Date
pub

Book
numt

Please
anotl

DEPARTMENT OF ENGLISH LOCAL HISTORY

OCCASIONAL PAPERS

Second Series

EDITED BY ALAN EVERITT

Number 4

The Pattern of Rural Dissent:
the Nineteenth Century

by

ALAN EVERITT

M.A., Ph.D., F.R.Hist.S.

Hatton Professor of English Local History
in the University of Leicester

LEICESTER UNIVERSITY PRESS

1972

BIBL. LONDIN. UNIV. SHL WITHDRAWN

First published in 1972 by
Leicester University Press

Distributed in North America by
Humanities Press Inc., New York

Copyright © Alan Everitt 1972

All rights reserved. No part of this publication
may be reproduced, stored in a retrieval system,
or transmitted, in any form or by any means,
electronic, mechanical, photocopying, recording, or otherwise,
without the prior permission of the Leicester University Press.

Set in Monotype Baskerville
Printed in Great Britain at
The Broadwater Press, Welwyn Garden City, Hertfordshire

ISBN 0 7185 2028 9

This volume is published with
the help of a grant from the late
Miss Isobel Thornley's Bequest
to the University of London

CONTENTS

ACKNOWLEDGEMENTS

Amongst the friends and colleagues to whom I am most indebted for information and advice in compiling this paper, I must particularly thank Dr John Walsh of Jesus College, Oxford, for his patience in reading and commenting upon it, for drawing my attention to books and articles I was unaware of, and for saving a novice in this field from numerous errors. I am grateful, too, to my colleague, Dr David Hey, for comments and references, particularly about Nonconformity in South Yorkshire. I must also thank my secretary, Mrs Muriel Phillips, for her skill and ingenuity in interpreting a particularly confusing and intractable manuscript.

I INTRODUCTORY[1]

THE English have a genius for retaining the form of their institutions and traditions while transforming their substance. For a people not much given to hard thinking, this habit of mind creates a comfortable illusion of continuity and a welcome sense of safety in a dangerous world. We still have a parliament at Westminster; but it is doubtful if the earliest members of that body would recognize any reflection of themselves and their activities in the modern mother of representative assemblies. We still hear the words 'nonconformity' and 'dissent' bandied about, at times with wearisome iteration; but there is virtually no connexion between the current use of these terms and their original meaning in the great days of the Nonconformist tradition between the Restoration and the First World War. Nowadays, with the waning of religious experience, 'nonconformity' has tended to become a mere synonym for social or political iconoclasm. And this is a pity because there was much more to the genuine, historic tradition of English Dissent than politics or mere iconoclasm. There was also more to it than simple antagonism to the Establishment: yet another term whose meaning has in recent years been wrested from its historic context and prostituted to the ephemeral needs of pamphleteers.

At the height of their power, in the middle of the nineteenth century, Dissenters probably comprised nearly half the church-going population of England. In the north-eastern counties, Cornwall, Wales, and parts of the Midlands, they numbered more than half. It is impossible, in fact, to make any valid study of provincial society during the last three centuries without taking some account of Nonconformist traditions. Certainly many Victorian novelists recognized this fact. There is much about the life of Dissenting communities in the provincial novels of George Eliot, Mrs Gaskell, Margaret Oliphant, and Arnold Bennett; for each of them spoke out of their own personal experience.

Almost as remarkable as the numbers of Nonconformists during the nineteenth century was their extraordinary fissiparation into warring factions. True, the great majority of Dissenters (in most areas more than 95 per cent) belonged to one or other of the more orthodox branches of the three principal denominations, of Congregationalists, Baptists, and Methodists. Yet at no pre-

---

[1] Some of the early paragraphs of this paper and most of the section on boundary settlements in section II have already appeared in print in *Land, Church, and People: Essays presented to Professor H. P. R. Finberg* (*The Agricultural History Review*, XVIII, Supplement, 1970), under the title 'Nonconformity in Country Parishes'. The various parts of the paper bear closely upon one another and to omit the section on the Old Dissent altogether would impair its general theme. I am grateful to the editor of the *Review* for permission to reprint the relevant paragraphs.

vious period, not even during the Great Rebellion, had there been such an astonishing plethora of sects as in the mid-Victorian era. At the end of 1866 there were no fewer than 98 religious denominations recorded in the register of marriages in England and Wales, and this number did not include all that were known to exist. Some of these denominations, it is true, were merely different names for the same bodies, and many were intensely localized. Of those recorded in the 1851 census, for instance, as many as 33 comprised no more than a single place of worship, and seventeen others only two or three. Yet the variety of these sects and their vivid nomenclature come as something of an eye-opener to the student of provincial society. What can have been the peculiar tenets, some may ask, of the Hallelujah Band, the Christian Eliasites, the Free Grace Gospel Christians, the New Jerusalem Church, the Peculiar People, the Progressivists, the Recreative Religionists, the Wesleyan Reform Glory Band, and the Christians who Object to be Otherwise Designated? In a sceptical and self-conscious age like our own, such oddities must provoke a certain amount of mirth. Yet it would be a mistake not to sense behind the absurdity something of significance. Such extreme and frequent fissiparation, after all, underlines at a certain social level the restlessness of the Victorian conscience and the urgency of its quest for a more perfect society. As is well known, it was this intensity of mind amongst Dissenters generally that lay behind some of the more militant reform movements of the time, both political and social.

Since the First World War, Nonconformity has largely ceased to be the aggressive force in English life that it once was. The historian should be wary of saying that it can never become so again, for society rarely develops along regular lines, but proceeds by unpredictable fits and starts. It is not often possible to be certain that a human movement has reached the ultimate end of its allotted span of life. The power in recent years of the more extreme sects to attract numerous adherents to themselves, almost alone among Christian bodies outside the Roman Catholic Church, is one of the stranger vagaries of the times. Nevertheless, the more traditional Dissenting denominations may be said to have come to the end of a certain cycle or phase in their history by the early years of the twentieth century.

Popular judgement might be inclined to date the decline of Nonconformity rather earlier, for example from the days of Darwin's *The Origin of Species*. But in the absolute numbers of their adherents, the major Dissenting bodies, despite important ups and downs in their fortunes, generally continued to expand till long after Charles Darwin. In rural areas it is common to find chapels founded, rebuilt, or extended up to the last decades of Queen Victoria's reign. A lonely Primitive Methodist chapel on the windswept Pennines above Middleton-in-Teesdale, for example, originally built in 1842, was extended and refronted in

1888. The Wesleyan chapel at Naseby in Northamptonshire, first erected in 1825, was enlarged and 'restored' in 1871, while a new Sunday School, nearly as large as the chapel itself, was added as late as 1903.[1] These two examples may be taken as typical of hundreds of others in country districts all over England.

The history of Dissent is one that should therefore be of some interest to the student of local society in England. The predilection of large and growing sections of the population for a locally autonomous form of religion, unfettered by archbishops, popes, or presbyteries, is indeed one of the more striking pecularities – one might almost say perversities – of English provincial society from the days of Charles I to those of Edward VII. It is one of the many signs that local attachments, far from declining with the growth of national consciousness, were in many ways becoming stronger. True, by no means all the traditional English sects placed equal emphasis on the autonomy of the local chapel. Compared with the Congregationalists, the Wesleyans, for instance, have always been a highly organized body. Nevertheless the life of every dissenting sect was centred in the local chapel. Its enthusiasm was the enthusiasm of a nexus of local dynasties, sometimes closely inbred through generations of intermarriage. And without too great a stretch of the evidence, it may be said that the gradual waning of Dissent began with the growth of centralization – in government, in provincial society, and in the organization of Nonconformity itself – during the last fifty or sixty years.

The importance of Dissent in provincial life has, of course, long been recognized, and has given rise to a very considerable literature of a kind. It must be confessed, however, that, faced with the sagging shelves of chapel histories and Dissenting hagiographies, even the most intrepid historian with no *a priori* interest in the subject is apt to wilt. Is it really possible to make useful generalizations out of this edifying literature, or to harness its not inconsiderable scholarship to the interests of a more secular age? The work of scholars like Dr G. F. Nuttall has shown that it certainly is.[2] In recent years a crop of university theses and many local studies have been devoted to various aspects of Nonconformity.[3] The present paper makes no attempt to synthesize this work or to explore the deeper spiritual problems of Dissenting history. It sets out with the limited aim of answering a single elementary question: in what types of rural community did Dissent tend to find a foothold and flourish? Was

[1] This information is from the datestones on the buildings. It must be added, however, that though absolute figures normally continued to increase, the Nonconformist *proportion* of the total population declined in some denominations and districts.

[2] See, for example, Dr Nuttall's article 'Dissenting Churches in Kent before 1700', *Journal of Ecclesiastical History*, XIV (1963), 175–89.

[3] Mr H. G. Tibbutt, for example, has published a series of studies in Bedfordshire Nonconformity, each devoted to the history of a local Congregational or Baptist church.

there any relationship between the differing species of local society and the proliferation of Dissent in certain well-defined areas, or its relative absence in others?[1]

Four counties have principally been examined in the following study: Northamptonshire, Leicestershire, Lincolnshire (more particularly Lindsey), and Kent. The aim has not been so much to explain differences between the four counties as differences within them. It may be remarked, however, that differences between them were also striking. In Lincolnshire, for example, to judge from the number of church and chapel 'sittings' recorded in the census of 1851, almost exactly half the church-going population were then Nonconformists.[2] This was an exceptionally high proportion, exceeded only in Cornwall, Bedfordshire, and the north-eastern counties, though it was nearly equalled in a few other shires with figures of 47–49 per cent. Despite the extraordinary number of medieval parishes in Lincolnshire – more than 600 – there were in fact many more Dissenting chapels there in the mid-nineteenth century than Anglican churches, to be precise 831 to 657. In Victorian Kent, by contrast, Nonconformists (judging again by 'sittings') numbered little more than a third of the church-going population (35 per cent), whereas Anglicans comprised almost two-thirds: and this despite the relatively rapid growth of population in this county, a development which usually encouraged the proliferation of Dissent.

Many other regional differences existed between the various persuasions in

[1] It is important to note in this connexion that, in the late seventeenth and early eighteenth centuries, certain rural chapels clearly acted as *regional* as well as local centres of Nonconformity. This seems to have been true in Bedfordshire, Cambridgeshire, Northamptonshire, the West Country, and Kent (cf. G. F. Nuttall, 'Dissenting Churches in Kent before 1700', *Journal of Ecclesiastical History*, XIV (1963), 181 and n.). The church-book of the Baptist chapel at Arnesby, Leicestershire (Leics. Record Office) shows that in the late seventeenth and early eighteenth centuries many members came from other villages and from places as far distant as Coventry and Ramsey (Huntingdonshire). This was one means, of course, by which the vitality of a sect might be maintained at a time and in a district where its members formed only a very small minority of the population. It is unlikely that those members who came from far afield attended the chapel regularly, week by week. More probably they were received simply as occasional visitors, a common custom in some Victorian sects. Nineteenth-century rural chapels sometimes had quite extensive stabling attached to them and some members evidently came from several miles away. In this context the periodic 'tea-meetings' common in some denominations, at which the members of a group of neighbouring chapels met together, no doubt often arriving on horseback, must not be forgotten.

[2] The census of 1851 was the only one that recorded religious adherence. For a discussion of the significance, reliability, and limitations of the census record see Professor K. S. Inglis's important article, 'Patterns of Religious Worship in 1851', *Journal of Ecclesiastical History*, XI (1960), 74–86. The value of the religious information in the census was much disputed at the time; but I accept the cogent and balanced case Professor Inglis advances (75–8), that on the whole it was conscientiously compiled and within its limits substantially reliable. For this paper I have principally relied on the summaries and abstracts of the census given under each county and parish entry in J. M. Wilson, *The Imperial Gazetteer of England and Wales*, 6 vols. (1870), (hereafter cited as *Imp. Gaz.*).

the four counties, some of which raise a number of intriguing questions.[1] Why was it, for example, that a West Country sect like the Bible Christians, intensely emotional and proletarian in character, found no adherents at all in three of these four counties, but more than 3,000 in Kent? (They were also numerous in Hampshire, but few in number in other southern counties, such as Sussex, Surrey, and Dorset.) Why was it that the more colourful or unusual sects – Latter-day Saints, Huntingtonians, Catholic and Apostolic Church, and a whole crop of nameless 'isolated congregations' – generally found far more followers in Kent than in the other three counties?[2] And why were there more than 20,000 Particular Baptists in both Kent and Northamptonshire, whereas there were only 7,000 in Leicestershire and less than 5,000 in Lincolnshire?[3] Such seemingly anomalous facts, however trivial they may appear to a secular age, are certainly in some way related to significant differences of local society as well as to more purely personal and spiritual causes. One does not need any profound knowledge of history, or any extensive acquaintance with chapel architecture, to recognize a certain social distinction between, say, the Primitive Methodists and the Wesleyans of Victorian England.[4] More intensive study of differences like these would undoubtedly point up many peculiarities in each region and sect. In the space of this paper they can only be mentioned in passing, in the hope that others may be encouraged to pursue them further.

[1] There is a good deal of suggestive information on the regional distribution of Nonconformity in Henry Pelling, *Social Geography of British Elections, 1885–1910* (1967). This is not the place to enter on a critique of this study, though I have reservations about some of Mr Pelling's conclusions. His purpose – the explanation of political behaviour – is of course different from mine in this paper, and he obviously views the evidence from a different angle. His book deals with broad regions rather than local communities, and for the present study his comments are rather too generalized to be of much assistance. It cannot be too strongly emphasized that the structure of a large number of individual local communities in any given region needs to be studied before any valid generalizations about the region itself can be advanced. As this paper attempts to show, local variations in parish type are often of more importance in the distribution of rural Dissent than regional differences. The regional divisions adopted by Mr Pelling (from C. B. Fawcett's *Provinces of England* (1919)) are in any case in some respects of doubtful validity from a historical point of view, particularly for the period before about 1860.

[2] Dissenters outside the three traditional bodies (Congregationalists, Baptists, Methodists) were three times as numerous as in the other counties.

[3] The strength of the Bapist churches in Kent has long been recognized. Only in Kent, in the seventeenth century, did they outnumber all other Dissenters. The county has been called, in fact, "a museum of Baptist antiquity" (cf. Nuttall, *op. cit.*, 181, quoting the Baptist historian W. T. Whitley). Dr Nuttall has shown that this strength dates back to the mid-seventeenth century if not before. The remarkable fact about the early Baptist traditions of the county, however, is that they were Arminian and not Calvinist. The growth by 1851 of the Particular Baptists, who were Calvinistic, must therefore have a different origin: there was very little connexion between the two branches of the Baptist faith.

[4] These are illustrated in the chapels of these two persuasions in many small towns and villages, for example at Old Bolingbroke (Lincolnshire) and Bottesford (Leicestershire). Rural Primitive Methodist chapels are often primitive indeed, and usually very small.

A suggestive attempt to explain certain geographical differences between the three major denominations (in particular Methodism) has been made by Dr Robert Currie in his important article 'A Micro-Theory of Methodist Growth'.[1] One of Dr Currie's most interesting comments relates to the contrast between generally Methodist areas and areas where the Congregationalist and Baptist denominations flourished. With certain exceptions, he remarks, "whilst the older dissent generally grew strong where the Church of England was strong, deriving (at least historically) much of its membership directly from the Church of England, Methodism grew strong where the Church of England was weak, and recruited from those sections of the population that Anglicanism failed to reach."[2] In a general way, the figures for 1851 certainly do appear to indicate that the Old Dissent was particularly associated with counties such as Northamptonshire, where parish churches were relatively numerous and Anglicanism in this sense was most powerful: whereas Methodism prospered particularly in counties like Durham where parish churches were relatively few and far between. Yet so far as rural areas are concerned the present writer confesses to some hesitation in accepting Dr Currie's generalization.[3]

In the first place it is difficult to ignore some of the striking exceptions to the rule, such as Lincolnshire. In this county there were more ancient parish churches than in any other except Norfolk, yet the Old Dissent was unusually weak and Methodism extraordinarily strong. Secondly, when the *local* distribution of the Old Dissent as between the different agrarian regions of a particular county is examined, it is evident that it most frequently took root in dis-

---

[1] *Proceedings of the Wesley Historical Society*, xxxvi (1967), 65–73. It should be pointed out that Dr Currie's article is not solely concerned with this problem, but ranges widely over questions of Methodist expansion and contraction generally.

[2] *Ibid.*, 68.

[3] There are in fact some difficult problems of definition involved in Dr Currie's analysis. These need not be followed up in detail here; but, to take one instance, it may be questioned whether the *county* unit on which his figures are principally based is normally a valid one for a comparative study of religious adherence, unless the differences between various parts of the same county are also taken into account. For example in Surrey it is hard to feel that in 1851 there can have been any real similarity between social and religious conditions in Bermondsey and Chiddingfold; or in Northumberland between Newcastle and Norham; or in Warwickshire between Birmingham and Shipston-on-Stour; or in Lancashire between Manchester and Coniston. The significant units of study in this context are surely the *type of local community* and the *type of economy in the region*. The same criticisms apply to Dr John D. Gay's very interesting recent book, *The Geography of Religion in England* (1971). This volume has appeared since the present paper was written and it is impossible to enter into an adequate critique of it in these pages. The most valuable part of it is the map section (pp. 264–325). Like Dr Currie, Dr Gay uses the *county* as his basic unit of study (cf. p. 51). To be fair, this is almost inevitable in a work covering the geography of religion in the whole of England over a period of more than three centuries. The historical sections of the book, though in places most suggestive, are not entirely satisfactory, and are not always adequately documented.

tricts where parishes were large and churches comparatively few in number. In the rural areas of Kent where Anglican churches were most numerous, namely the Downlands, the Old Dissent rarely established itself. Its stronghold was in the very large parishes of the Weald, where country people often had several miles to walk to reach their church. The stronghold of rural Methodism, by contrast, was principally in areas where parish churches were relatively numerous, in particular on the chalk Downlands. A somewhat similar pattern may be observed in Leicestershire, where the Old Dissent was most powerful in the relatively large and scattered wood-pasture parishes in the west of the county, whereas Methodism often took root in the small limestone parishes in the east of the county. It is possible, of course, that these three shires – Lincolnshire, Leicestershire, and Kent – were all untypical of the rest of England; but the same kind of development has been observed by Dr David Hey in South Yorkshire, and one suspects that detailed local analysis would show that this pattern was not an uncommon one. If this is so it seems at least as true of the Old Dissent as of Methodism that in rural areas it most frequently fitted into the gaps left by Anglicanism. It was not a peculiarity of Methodism to be particularly successful "in the out-townships of straggling parishes",[1] but a characteristic of Dissenting bodies generally. The fact that the New Dissent was much stronger than the Old in counties like Durham where Anglican churches were comparatively few must be due to other causes than simply the numerical weakness of Anglicanism.

The purpose of these remarks is not to criticize an attempt to explain large-scale regional differences between the different denominations such as Dr Currie refers to. These differences are of great interest and significance and there is no need to minimize them. In the present writer's view, however, it is essential first of all to explore the smaller, more localized differences *within* each shire. No English county is entirely homogeneous in its forms of parochial society. Each comprises a number of diverse sub-regions or rural economies within it, and a varied spectrum of parish types. In each of the four counties under consideration there co-existed, in different guises and degrees, a somewhat similar spectrum of parish types and some at least of the same kinds of rural economy. And the significant fact is that in each county Dissent tended to be associated chiefly with certain forms of local society, while it was largely absent from others. In a recent paper the present writer attempted to relate the distribution of Dissent in its earlier phases, before the Evangelical Revival, to these varying forms of local society.[2] The present paper seeks to trace a similar

---

[1] Currie, *op. cit.*, 69, citing B. Greaves, *An Analysis of the Spread of Methodism in Yorkshire . . .*, Leeds University thesis (1961).

[2] Everitt, 'Nonconformity in Country Parishes', *loc. cit.*

relationship at a later date, after the impact of Evangelicalism, amongst other developments, had revolutionized the place of Nonconformity in English life. In the first part of the paper the different forms of parish and village in the four counties are examined in this connotation, and in the later part the peculiar characteristics of each county individually.

At this point perhaps a preliminary word of warning is necessary. The present writer does not believe that all differences in the distribution of Dissent can be explained in terms of diverse rural economies. If it were possible to examine in microscopic detail the complete social and familial structure of every local and regional community represented in this study, the whole tangled nexus of geological, geographical, climatic, topographical, racial, economic, cultural, and religious factors in their development, it would doubtless be possible to explain some of the puzzles to which the present paper affords no solution. We might then know why nearly half the population of Lincolnshire appears to have been Nonconformist in 1851 whilst only one-third of that of Kent comes in this category. Yet the probability remains that many peculiarities in the pattern of Dissent would still elude us, for much was certainly due to purely personal or fortuitous causes.

The fortunes of a chapel could easily be wrecked, for example, by the development of a local family feud. A Dissenting group might be prevented from forming by the presence of a dominating personality in the place. Its growth might be retarded or even terminated merely by the absence of anyone with sufficient education or force of character to take a vital decision at a critical juncture. (The influence of the single forceful individual or family is a recurring theme in the fortunes of most Nonconformist chapels.) Conversely, the local influence of a particular religious group might be greatly extended by the visits of a powerful preacher from a neighbouring town or village. And of course much undoubtedly depended upon the attitude and energy of the local Anglican parson. In many cases there was a definite campaign on the part of the parson to stamp out Nonconformity in his parish; but this was by no means the only way in which Anglican influence retarded the growth of Dissent. Was there not often, perhaps, less of a tendency for it to develop where the rector himself was strongly Evangelical? Had not secession sometimes taken place in the eighteenth century largely because of the laxity of a latitudinarian or pluralist? Had it not sometimes been forestalled by the timely arrival of an ardent Evangelical capable of meeting the new demand for a more 'vital' religious life? Was is not often fostered, when the Evangelical era gave way to the Tractarian, by the arrival of a youthful and intolerant Puseyite in place of the old Protestant vicar? Certainly there is much in the literature of the time to support these views. In the limits of this paper, however, attention has rather been focused on what may loosely be termed some of the sociological influences in the pattern of rural Dissent, whilst the influence of personalities has been left to others to explore.

II   RURAL SOCIETY AND DISSENT

NONCONFORMITY in the nineteenth century was altogether different in scale from Nonconformity in the seventeenth.[1] At the time of the Compton Census in 1676, in the two dioceses of Canterbury and Rochester Dissenters numbered less than 10 per cent of the population; yet they are said to have been unusually numerous in this area.[2] True, the 1670s were a period of persecution, and the Compton Census has serious limitations as a historical source. Yet the general tenor of the evidence suggests that, with some notable exceptions, most Nonconformist groups remained relatively small and sparse until the middle of the eighteenth century. They exerted an influence in English society out of all proportion to their modest numbers; yet the days of great 'revivals' and mass 'conversions' still lay in the future.

By the 1850s Dissenters were not only far more numerous than ever before but had come to form a far larger proportion of the population. This is clear from the census of 1851, the first and only one to record religious allegiance. In most counties Dissenters appear to have comprised by this date at least a third of the church-going population.[3] In Cornwall and the north-east they actually outnumbered Anglicans. In Teesdale, for instance, there were 17 Anglican churches in 1851, with 3,185 'sittings'; whereas there were 28 Methodist chapels, with 4,577 sittings, and 38 Nonconformist chapels altogether, capable of accommodating more than 6,500 people. Even in a southern county like Kent, where by this date Dissent was a good deal weaker than in the north-east, there were 500 Nonconformist chapels, compared with 479 Anglican

[1] In 1672–3 licences were taken out for Presbyterian meeting-houses in 32 Kentish parishes, for Baptists in 21, and for Independents in 11.—C. W. Chalklin, *Seventeenth-Century Kent: a Social and Economic History* (1965), 227. These figures should be compared with the total of 500 Nonconformist chapels in Kent recorded in the 1851 census. The typical congregation was usually smaller, moreover, in the seventeenth and early eighteenth centuries, not exceeding 40 or 50 members in many cases. For the membership of Dissenting chapels at this time see, for example, Margaret Spufford, 'The Dissenting Churches in Cambridgeshire from 1600–1700', *Proceedings of the Cambridge Antiquarian Society*, LXI (1968); Thomas Coleman, *Memorials of the Independent Churches in Northamptonshire* (1853), *passim*; Chalklin, *Seventeenth-Century Kent*, 227, mentions congregations at Deptford of about 50 and at Ashford of about 30 in the 1670s. However, some (usually urban) *congregations*, no doubt including many people who were not formal church members, were probably much larger than this. Dr G. F. Nuttall (*op. cit.*, 177–8, 187) cites contemporary references to congregations of 200 or 300, 700, 300 or 400, 300, and 200 in Canterbury, Dover, Deal, Faversham, Staplehurst, and Leeds (Kent).

[2] See Appendix, Table I.   [3] See Appendix, Table II.

churches.[1] These figures must not be interpreted as statistics of membership, of course. Dissenting chapels were at this date usually smaller than churches, and we do not know how many seats were in fact regularly occupied. Nevertheless it is indisputable that, by 1851, Nonconformists comprised a far more powerful section of the population than ever before.[2]

As remarked above, the 1851 census was the first and last to record religious allegiance. The disputes and quarrels about its reliability were at the time notorious, and formed the major reason why no subsequent record was attempted. A balanced and thorough examination of the uses and limitations of the census figures is given in K. S. Inglis, 'Patterns of Religious Worship in 1851' (see note 2 on page 8). Professor Inglis concludes by agreeing with *The Times* of the day that "the result may be taken as substantially accurate and trustworthy." From my own researches for this paper I would endorse Professor Inglis's view.

The census recorded (a) the number of churches and chapels; (b) the number of 'sittings' in churches and chapels; and (c) the actual attendance in church and chapel on census Sunday. There are obvious objections to the figures for both (b) and (c) as a basis for statistical analysis. But in view of the fact that attendance was generally said to be a good deal lower than normal on census Sunday and was lower in some areas than others, it has seemed best, for the present purpose, to use the statistics of 'sittings' rather than of 'attendance'. The former, it is true, can give only a rough and ready guide to membership. For various reasons the figures of 'sittings' are probably more misleading for Anglicans than Dissenters. In East Anglia, for example, they probably exaggerate Anglican strength because of the number and size of ancient parish churches in this area, as compared with, say, Lancashire and the West Riding. With all their defects, however, the 1851 figures are the best we have. In the four counties principally studied for this paper (Leicestershire, Lincolnshire, Northamptonshire, and Kent) they do not seem likely to be seriously misleading. When the census tells us that there were 221 Primitive Methodist chapels in Lincolnshire with 25,164 sittings, but only 16 in Northamptonshire with 1,759 sittings, we need not assume that these figures exactly represent the local strength of Primitive Methodism; but they do furnish a rough guide to its comparative predominance, and point up important differences between the two counties.

[1] *Imp. Gaz.*, *sub* Teesdale, Kent.

[2] As explained above (p. 8 n. 2), for this paper I have in general utilized the abstracts of census figures recorded in *The Imperial Gazetteer* (1870). Probably because it was compiled by a Scot, this gazetteer is generally remarkable for the variety and reliability of its statistical information. It is on the whole a good deal more thorough and scholarly than Lewis's *Gazetteer* (1833) or *The National Gazetteer* (1868), though these supplement *The Imperial Gazetteer* in certain respects.

In the past the attendance figures have been more frequently made use of than those of chapels and 'sittings'. Briefly, the problems in utilizing the attendance figures may be summarized as follows. First, census Sunday coincided with a period of unusually severe weather, which was said to have kept many people away from church who normally attended, particularly in the northern counties: a fact that must invalidate regional comparison of attendance figures to some extent, particularly where very large parishes are concerned. Secondly, census Sunday also coincided with a period of unusually widespread illness, again reducing the attendance below normal, in some areas apparently more than others. Thirdly, though the figures for attendants at each service on census Sunday are given, there is no certain way of estimating the *real total* of attendants, since we do not know how many who attended in the afternoon or evening had also been present at an earlier service. It was said at the time that Dissenters more often attended two or even three services than Anglicans. If this was correct (and it quite probably was) the *total* of attendants at all three services would exaggerate the real strength of Dissent at the expense of the Anglican church. Various ways of circumventing this particular problem have been suggested but none of them seem entirely satisfactory. Fourthly, many clergy (particularly in some dioceses of the Church of England) refused to comply with the census requirement and for their churches there are no reliable attendance figures, though estimates were made by the enumerators. Finally, many members of some Dissenting denominations are said to have also attended services in their parish church, usually no doubt at times when there was no service in their own chapel. These will appear as Anglicans in attendance figures, of course, and there is no way of estimating their numbers.

Throughout the following study Roman Catholics and Jews have been excluded. Both groups are special cases and as a rule they formed at this date a very small minority of the population. Their inclusion would not, in fact, have materially affected the statistics. The 'sittings' for the two bodies respectively in the four counties were: Kent 3,337 Roman Catholics (13 places of worship), and 315 Jews (5 places of worship); Leicestershire 2,537 (12), and *nil*; Lincolnshire 2,019 (13), and *nil*; Northamptonshire 705 (6), and *nil*. Roman Catholics thus formed 1 per cent of the church-going population in Kent (judged by number of 'sittings'), 1·6 per cent in Leicestershire, 0·7 per cent in Lincolnshire, and 0·5 per cent in Northamptonshire. Traditionally Lancashire is always thought of as a 'Catholic' county, and it was certainly more so than any other. But in 1851 there were in fact only 55,610 Roman Catholic 'sittings' in the county, compared with 324,751 Nonconformists and 383,466 Anglicans. Even in Lancashire Catholics were, in fact, greatly outnumbered by both Congregationalists (80,072 sittings) and Wesleyan Methodists (107,983 sittings). This fact alone is symptomatic of the enormous extension of Nonconformity by the year 1851.

The principal factor in the growth of Nonconformity in the century preceding 1851 had been the Evangelical Awakening. The Methodists, as is well known, owed their origin to the Awakening, and by 1851 they were almost everywhere the most numerous Dissenting body. Even in southern counties like Kent and Sussex the disciples of Wesley comprised about 40 per cent of all Dissenters; and in Lincolnshire Methodists were nearly three times as numerous as all other Dissenting groups put together. The impact of the Evangelical Movement was not confined to Methodists, however.[1] Its earliest origins may perhaps be said to have taken their rise amongst the Independents and the Moravian Brethren. If any event can be regarded as beginning the Evangelical Movement it is probably the appointment of the Independent Philip Doddridge to Castle Hill Chapel in Northampton in 1729, and the transference of his Academy to the same town in that year. These events antedated the conversion of John Wesley by nine years, and the quiet but far-reaching influence of Doddridge, by means of his teaching, his writings, and his hymns, prepared the way for the reception of the new Movement amongst all sections and classes of provincial society.[2] By Queen Victoria's reign virtually every Dissenting sect and the Church of England itself had been largely transformed by it. By and large, however, it was probably the Dissenters as a whole who gained most: Congregationalists, Baptists, Methodists, and a dozen other smaller communions.

Nonconformity, like Puritanism, has often been thought of as a predominantly urban phenomenon, but it is doubtful if any essential connexion with urban society can be substantiated.[3] Certainly in the seventeenth and early

---

[1] Sects inimical to Evangelicalism, like the Presbyterians in Kent, evidently declined in the late eighteenth century. Edward Hasted more than once remarks on this phenomenon at this time: "The Presbyterians formerly were the most numerous sect throughout this county; but they are greatly diminished of late years, and the Methodistical Baptists are the prevailing sect, and greatly increasing every year through every part of it."—*The History and Topographical Survey of the County of Kent*, 2nd edn (1797–1801), VII, 93.

[2] These remarks are based on the author's as yet unpublished research on Doddridge's work at Northampton and his writings. I owe a great debt in this to Dr G. F. Nuttall, whose publications on Doddridge are invaluable, in particular his contributions to the bicentenary volume edited by him, *Philip Doddridge, 1702–51: his Contribution to English Religion* (1955). Doddridge's most influential works, it should be said, came after 1729: *The Family Expositor*, vol. I, in 1739, and *The Rise and Progress of Religion in the Soul* in 1745. The first collected edition of his hymns (written at many dates during his ministry) was not published till 1753, after his death. This went through eight editions in the next 39 years. Doddridge and Watts are usually regarded as the real founders of English hymnody.

[3] Dr John Gay seems to me to overstress this urban element. He remarks, for example, that "English country life [as distinct from urban life] was not divided on matters of religion until the coming of

eighteenth centuries a great deal of Dissent was based in the countryside.[1] In many towns, it is true, such as Canterbury, Maidstone, Dover, and Northampton, Dissent was a powerful force, and possibly in most more forceful and vociferous than its mere numbers might lead us to expect. It was also, of course, very powerful in London. But if one analyses sources like the subscribers' lists of celebrated Dissenting works in the early eighteenth century, one is likely to find that the truly urban subscribers were considerably outnumbered by those from purely agricultural areas and small market centres. Of the 1,100 subscribers to the first volume of Philip Doddridge's *magnum opus*, *The Family Expositor* (1739), only 2 per cent came from London (where it was published) and 35 per cent from the larger provincial towns like Coventry, Liverpool, Hull, Oxford, Shrewsbury, and Bristol. By contrast 34 per cent came from very small rural market centres like Olney, Oundle, and Cullompton, and nearly 30 per cent from wholly agrarian parishes. Many of the 'urban' subscriptions, moreover, probably represented country people, since they came from booksellers in market towns, whose customers doubtless included villagers as well as townsmen. Probably at least two-thirds of the subscribers, therefore, were really of rural or semi-rural origin.

The country basis of much of the Old Dissent may be further illustrated from the numbers of Nonconformists recorded under each parish in the Compton Census of 1676. These figures cannot be regarded as exact statistics; in some parishes it is clear that they were largely based upon guesswork. But they are the earliest general figures that we have, and broadly speaking they are confirmed by other types of evidence. For Kent the figures have been edited by Mr C. W. Chalklin, and the following calculations are based upon his text.[2] Of

John Wesley", except in Essex, Hertfordshire, and the South Midlands (*op. cit.*, p. 162, and cp. pp. 105, 108). This is too simple a view. Local studies like those of Mr R. H. Evans for Leicestershire (*Trans. of the Leics. Arch. Soc.*, xxv (1949), *passim*; xxviii (1952), p. 71) show that it was certainly not the case.

[1] Regarding the distribution of the 'Old Dissent', the influence of the Clarendon Code (particularly the Five Mile Act) in dispersing Dissent from the incorporated towns into the countryside obviously needs to be taken account of. The implementation of the Code, however, varied much from year to year, from sect to sect, and from county to county. Much depended on the local attitude of the J.P.s and their vigilance. In corporate towns like Leicester, Tenterden, Canterbury, and Northampton, Nonconformity was far from being extinguished by the Code. Licences for conventicles taken out under Charles II's Declaration of Indulgence were usually most numerous in these incorporated boroughs. Although, in total, there were probably more rural than urban Dissenters in most counties, many corporations remained Nonconformist strongholds. Northampton was the most important single centre of Dissent in Northamptonshire, and Canterbury, Maidstone, and Dover were amongst the most prominent in Kent. In the Weald the principal Dissenting parishes in the 1670s were Cranbrook and Tenterden, the latter a corporation, the former a large parish containing an unincorporated town and many subsidiary hamlets and outlying farms.

[2] C. W. Chalklin, 'The Compton Census of 1676: the Dioceses of Canterbury and Rochester', *Kent Records: a Seventeenth Century Miscellany*, Kent Archaeological Soc., Records Publication Committee,

the total of 7,037 Dissenters recorded in the county of Kent in 1676, 51 per cent came from wholly rural parishes and 49 per cent from the towns. These gross figures need some care, however, in interpretation. Included among the urban 'nonconformists' in Kent are also the members of foreign congregations (principally French-speaking) in Canterbury, Sandwich, Maidstone, and Dover. The numbers of these groups are not given separately in the census; but in the 1640s they appear to have exceeded 1,500.[1] Probably, therefore, a good third of the 3,464 urban 'nonconformists' in Kent must be excluded if we are to arrive at a true figure for the native, indigenous Dissenters. This leaves a total of 5,882 Nonconformists in the county as a whole, and of these 61 per cent lived in wholly agrarian parishes.[2]

By the time of the 1851 Census one would expect the urban element in Dissent to have expanded with the increase of town populations generally, and the rural proportion correspondingly to have declined. In a number of counties this development certainly appears to have taken place. Of the 500 Dissenting chapels in Kent recorded in the census of 1851 only 178 (36 per cent) were in rural parishes, whereas nearly two-thirds were now in urban communities. In some shires the decline in rural Nonconformity had begun long before the nineteenth century, though further research may reveal that this decline had been of a temporary nature. In Warwickshire Mrs Judith Hurwich has found evidence of a dramatic fall in numbers by the year 1720, when probably about two-thirds of Dissenters appear to have been townsmen in contrast with only about one-third in 1662.[3] Yet by 1851 in many counties the rural element in

---

XVII (1960), 153–74. For the following calculations I have excluded the three or four suburban parishes adjoining London, since properly these appertain to the metropolitan rather than the Kentish economy. It has usually been assumed in the past that the Compton figures refer only to communicants. It is now realized that they vary in their basis, but generally they include adults only. The problems of the reliability of this 'census' and the extent to which it underestimates Nonconformists cannot be discussed here. Its validity was seriously challenged in the 1920s by Dr T. Richards (*The Religious Census of 1676: an Inquiry into its Historical Value, mainly in Reference to Wales*, Cymmrodorion Society, 1927); but Mr Chalklin shows that his strictures, so far as Kent was concerned, were exaggerated. It must be admitted that the membership of early Nonconformist churches in counties like Northamptonshire, Kent, and Cambridgeshire seems to have been very small, rarely as high as 50. But the real problem is the unknown number of 'occasional conformists', and the extent to which these should be reckoned as 'Dissenters' or 'Anglicans'.

[1] There were 900 in Canterbury, 500 in Sandwich, and 50 in Maidstone, according to a contemporary account (British Museum, Thomason Tracts, E.285.6, p. 22). The figure for Dover is not given.

[2] This figure probably underestimates the total, since many 'urban' parishes in Kent (e.g., Maidstone and Cranbrook) included thousands of acres of countryside with subsidiary villages and hamlets. We do not know how many Nonconformists in these places were in fact countrymen, and I have therefore reckoned all as 'urban'. In emphasizing the strength of urban Dissent in Kent Mr Chalklin (*op. cit.*, 173–4) seems to have overlooked this fact. He has also included the foreign congregations as well as indigenous Dissenters in his remarks.

[3] I am much indebted to Mrs Hurwich for this information. Her figures, based on the place of

Nonconformity had either regained much of its former preponderance or else had always remained as powerful as the urban. Nearly two-thirds of the 841 chapels in Northamptonshire and Lindsey at this time were in country parishes, and in Leicestershire the proportion was nearly 70 per cent.[1] True, the typical rural chapel was often smaller than its urban counterpart; yet it can hardly be denied that Nonconformity remained exceedingly powerful in many country districts of Victorian England. There are still hundreds of chapels in the rural parishes of counties like Lincolnshire, Leicestershire, Northamptonshire, Norfolk, and Devon bearing witness to the strength of rural Dissent at this time, though many are now pathetically derelict.

What relation did the new pattern of Dissent, in the rural England of Queen Victoria's reign, bear to the original pattern of the seventeenth century? Very often it was associated with the same forms of rural economy as before. In Kent and Sussex, for instance, the Weald remained the classic area of local Nonconformity, and forest societies elsewhere also continued to encourage its proliferation. As early as 1661 it had been said that "the Wild of Kent is a receptacle for distressed running parsons, who vent abundance of sedition;"[2] and in the nineteenth century it remained very powerful in the old centres like Cranbrook, Staplehurst, and Tenterden. By 1851, however, Dissenters were also numerous in other types of local community. In Kent they were now by no means peculiar to the Weald, but were powerful in a number of downland parishes like Elham and Meopham. At the time of the Compton Census there had been only one downland parish in Kent (Ripple, near Dover) with more than 20 Nonconformists; by 1851 chapels had sprung up in many others, and in a few there were two or three. In east Leicestershire, too, where Dissent had hitherto been

residence of 1,390 Dissenters between 1662 and 1720, show that 35 per cent were 'urban' in 1662, 31 per cent in 1683, 49 per cent in 1700, and 68 per cent in 1720. Mrs Hurwich adds that in some respects these figures probably exaggerate the urban element, but that other evidence, such as the number and location of meeting-places, clearly indicates that in Warwickshire Dissent had become markedly more urban by 1720. The same development may have taken place in Kent. In 1690–2 the estimated numbers of 'auditors' of Congregational and Presbyterian ministers in Kentish towns were as follows: Canterbury 900 to 1,000; Dover 700; Maidstone 700; Rochester 500; Sandwich 400; Deal 300 to 400; Faversham 300 (Nuttall, 'Dissenting Churches', *loc. cit.*, 177–8, 186–7). These figures, estimated from the Nonconformist viewpoint, seem suspiciously rounded, and of course 'auditors' were not necessarily identical with communicant members. Moreover, the town congregations may have included many auditors from surrounding villages (this was the case in other towns, such as Northampton), and a number of rural congregations were also surprisingly large in the 1690s: for example 300 at Staplehurst, 400 to 500 at Goudhurst. Nevertheless, there seem strong grounds for suspecting a pronounced (if perhaps only temporary) growth in the urban element in Nonconformity in Kent at this date, as in Warwickshire.

[1] See Appendix, Table XXII.

[2] Nuttall, 'Dissenting Churches', *loc. cit.*, 185, quoting V.C.H., *Kent*, .., 100. Fenland areas were also traditionally conducive to Dissent, for example on the Yorkshire/Lincolnshire borders around Haxey.

comparatively weak, Methodist chapels had been established by 1851 in many country parishes. Most striking of all was the difference in a county like Lincolnshire. This was an area with no considerable forest tracts, and, it seems, comparatively little Dissent before the eighteenth century. Yet by 1851 Dissenters had come close to outnumbering Anglicans. How can we explain this new layer in the palimpsest of Nonconformity? In what types of rural parish and of rural economy had the New Dissent taken root?

Freeholders' Parishes

Glancing one day through the pages of the *Imperial Gazetteer*, published in 1870, the present writer noticed almost by chance that Dissenting chapels often seemed to be associated with parishes where the property was described as 'divided' or 'much subdivided'.[1] The information about Dissent in the *Gazetteer* was based upon the Census of 1851, and that about property-holding upon the Return of 1860.[2] This chance observation led to a more thorough investigation of the relationship between patterns of landownership and the distribution of Dissent. For this purpose four counties were selected, chiefly because of some general acquaintance with their historical economy: Leicestershire, Northamptonshire, Lindsey, and Kent. Whether or not the resemblances and contrasts between the four counties ultimately prove to be typical of England as a whole, and however they are interpreted, they appear to be too striking to be overlooked.

Altogether there were 1,343 parishes in these four counties, but for 111 of them the information about landownership was inadequate, and these had to be omitted. The analysis of the remaining 1,232 parishes is summarized in the Appendix to this paper.[3] Broadly speaking, the property in each parish is described in the Return as either 'in one hand', 'in a few hands', 'subdivided', or 'much subdivided'. For the sake of simplicity in the present argument the two former classes may be broadly grouped together under the name of 'estate parishes', since in these all the land appears to have been held by a single magnate or a few dominant landowners: whilst the two latter classes, where land was divided amongst many proprietors, may be grouped under the designation 'freeholders' parishes', since they evidently contained many small and inde-

[1] Since writing the above, I find that Dr Dennis Mills briefly pointed out the same association in 'English Villages in the Eighteenth and Nineteenth Centuries: a Sociological Approach', *Amateur Historian*, VI (1963–5), 277. Dr John Gay (*op. cit.*, p. 111) also briefly alludes to the association of Dissent with the 'open' villages where there was no dominant landlord. His further remark that such villages were "economically poorer" is not necessarily true. They must often have had a far larger number of *moderately* prosperous inhabitants than estate villages.

[2] *Imp. Gaz.*, III, Preface (at end of vol.), p. v.   [3] See Appendix, Tables III and IV.

pendent owners.[1] This rough and ready division obviously glosses over with deceptive simplicity what was in fact a highly complex pattern of landowner-ship. But for a generalized survey like the present a minute examination of the structure of landowning in more than 1,200 parishes would clearly have been impracticable.

Within the economy of each of the four counties, the predominant influence of landownership upon the spread of Nonconformity is very evident. Table III analyses the parishes in each shire by *type of property-holding*. The third division of the table, headed Total of I and II, represents all the 'estate parishes', where there was a single landlord or a few dominant squires. In Kent 86 per cent of these estate parishes had no Dissenting chapel of any kind: in only 14 per cent was there any organized Nonconformity. In Lindsey the position was similar to that in Kent, with chapels in only 18 per cent of the estate parishes. In North-amptonshire and Leicestershire the absence of Dissent in this type of commu-nity was not quite so striking, the relevant figures being 25 per cent and 27 per cent respectively. In all four counties, however, Nonconformist chapels were very much the exception wherever land was concentrated in the hands of a few local magnates. In the case of parishes where all the land was controlled by a *single* magnate, Dissent hardly ever established a foothold. In only three of the 119 parishes in this category was there any form of organized Nonconformity. In these manorial domains, whatever else was permitted, no conventicle was allowed to rear its disturbing head.

Further down the table the section headed 'Total of III and IV' comprises all the 'freeholders' parishes', that is where land was 'subdivided' or 'much subdivided'. The contrast here is remarkable. In Kent there was at least one Dissenting chapel in 70 per cent of these parishes, and in 17 per cent of them there was more than one. In the more strongly Nonconformist counties of Northamptonshire, Leicestershire, and Lindsey the proportions were a good deal higher. In Northamptonshire chapels were to be found in 77 per cent of these freeholders' parishes, in Leicestershire in 83 per cent, and in Lindsey in 86 per cent. There were also many parishes in these three counties with two or three chapels, and some with four or five. In Northamptonshire there were two or more chapels in 42 per cent of the freeholders' parishes, in Leicestershire in 44 per cent, and in Lindsey in 61 per cent.

[1] Typologically, many freeholders' parishes bear a close resemblance to the 'open parishes' of Warwickshire described by Dr J. M. Martin in 'The Parliamentary Enclosure Movement and Rural Society in Warwickshire', *The Agricultural History Review*, xv, i (1967), 19–39. Of the 15 places specifi-cally mentioned as 'open parishes' by Dr Martin, at the time of enclosure, at least nine were still free-holders' settlements in 1860, and probably four others. Only two, it seems, were definitely 'estate parishes' by that date, with all their property in 'a few hands'—Binton and Brailes. See also p. 35, n. 2, *infra*.

The fourth table analyses the same information in a different way: by the *distribution of chapels* within each county. The first division of the table shows that in Kent estate parishes accounted for 78 per cent of those where there was no organized Dissent. In Leicestershire the proportion was rather higher, and in Northamptonshire and Lindsey it was nearly 90 per cent. Further down the table, by contrast, the section headed 'Total of II, III, and IV' comprises all the parishes where there were Nonconformist chapels. This shows that in Leicestershire, Lindsey, and Kent about three-quarters of these were free-holders' parishes. In Northamptonshire, it is interesting to note, the figure was markedly lower, no more than 60 per cent. This was evidently because, despite the growth of landed estates in the county and the decline in the number of freeholders' parishes, the tradition of Dissent sometimes remained powerful in villages where independent smallholdings had been engrossed by the aristo-cracy or squirearchy.

The fourth section of Table IV suggests that the greater the tendency to sub-division of land, the greater also was the tendency to Dissent. This section in-cludes all the parishes in each county with three or more chapels. The figures show that in Lindsey 73 per cent of these, in Leicestershire 76 per cent, and in Kent 89 per cent were parishes where land was not simply 'subdivided' but '*much* subdivided'.[1] (In Northamptonshire, once again, the proportion is noticeably lower, no more than 55 per cent.) The most extreme example of this proliferation of Dissent was Haxey, in Lindsey, where in 1851 there were no fewer than 12 different Methodist chapels. Even by Lincolnshire standards this was extraordinary; but there were nearly 40 other rural parishes in Lindsey with three or more Nonconformist churches, and 33 in Leicestershire. (These figures may be compared with 11 in Northamptonshire and nine in Kent.)[2]

Boundary Settlements

Though freeholders' parishes form perhaps the most obvious and numerous kind of rural society encouraging Dissent, they cannot always be invoked to explain its proliferation. Another form of society in which it tended to flourish was the frontier settlement, situated on the boundary between two parishes. Places of this kind tended to be particularly frequent in old forest districts, where wasteland was more abundant; but they were not confined to wood-lands. In Kent, where they were exceptionally numerous, they were to be

[1] There were only nine parishes altogether in Kent, however, with three or more chapels, so that the percentage in this case should not be overstressed.

[2] It is noteworthy that the proliferation of chapels was generally more marked in the Midlands than in Kent. In Northamptonshire there were 51 rural parishes with two or more chapels, in Leicestershire 62, and in Lindsey 110, compared with only 33 in Kent.

found here and there in most parts of the county. In Cowden, for example, a Wealden parish on the Sussex border, there are still nine outlying settlements situated on the parish boundary. In Lenham, a mid-Kent parish straddling the downs and the chartlands, the parish border passes through the middle of 11 distinct hamlets and farmhouses. In Elham, a large downland parish of East Kent, the boundary bisects no fewer than 13 subsidiary communities. The origins of these settlements are outside the scope of this paper; but most of them go back at least to the fourteenth century, and probably a good deal earlier; a few, indeed, are recorded in Anglo-Saxon charters. Seventeen or more of the 33 in these three parishes are mentioned in documents dating from before 1385, and many of the rest, on topographical or toponymic grounds, must probably be assigned to an equally early period.[1] Dissent was not found in more than a few of these boundary settlements, of course. Most of them have remained solitary farmsteads ever since their foundation. A number, however, at some period of their history, gradually developed into populous rural communities in their own right. In Kent these kinds of boundary settlement are often distinguished by characteristic suffixes, such as *common* (e.g., Goathurst Common, on the border of Sundridge and Chevening); or *minnis*, a Kentish word meaning 'land held in common' (e.g., Stelling Minnis and Rhodes Minnis); or *lees*, a word in Kentish usage often referring to 'rough commonland or pasture' (e.g., Challock Lees and Kennington Lees); or simply the word *green* (e.g., Grafty Green, on the border of Lenham and Boughton Monchelsea). Places like these were the kind of boundary settlements that often proved conducive to Dissent. Many, it will be noticed from their names, were situated on common land, shared between two or three parishes, where jurisdictions were difficult to define and tended to come into dispute. Such conditions often fostered independent or (according to one's viewpoint) lawless behaviour; for in such a community it was always easy, on the approach of the parish constable, to claim that the inhabitants in question were not under *his* jurisdiction but that of the next parish.

In Leicestershire a classic example of such a settlement is the village of Walton, a few miles east of Lutterworth. Nowadays the boundary has been adjusted to include the whole of Walton in Kimcote parish; but originally it passed through the middle of Walton village, so that half the settlement lay in Kimcote and half in Knaptoft. Walton is certainly an ancient settlement, for it is mentioned in Domesday, and is quite possibly older than either Knaptoft or Kimcote. It may have originated as a settlement of British serfs or slaves, for the name may mean 'the *tūn* of the Welshmen'. Or alternatively it may mean 'the

---

[1] J. K. Wallenberg, *Kentish Place-Names* (1931), *passim*; and *The Place-Names of Kent* (1934), 81–3, 223–7, 431–5.

tūn in a wood'. Either meaning would explain its subsidiary relationship to Kimcote and Knaptoft, of which it has remained an outlying appendage, with no parish church of its own even today, though in medieval times there was a chapel. Yet it was large enough to develop a strong community life, with several times the population of Kimcote and many times that of the now vanished village of Knaptoft. In George III's reign there were a number of shopkeepers and craftsmen among its inhabitants, and probably many more framework-knitters than farmworkers. How far back the Nonconformist traditions of this boundary settlement go we do not know; but during Queen Victoria's reign there were two Dissenting groups within it, whereas there were none in either Knaptoft or Kimcote.[1]

Another, though much later, example of a Leicestershire boundary settlement with a strong Dissenting tradition is Coalville. It originated in the 1820s, under the name of Long Lane, at the junction of three distinct parishes, Ibstock, Whitwick, and Packington, and the separate chapelry of Snibston. By 1838 its first Nonconformist chapel had been erected, by the Baptists, and by 1870 (with a population of about 1,700) there were no fewer than four dissenting churches, with but a single place of worship for Anglicans.[2] No doubt other factors than its situation at the junction of three parishes affected Coalville's propensity to Dissent; yet it is interesting as an unusually late example of the persistent association between Nonconformity and boundary societies.

Closely similar in character to these boundary settlements were those which sprang up on extra-parochial tracts and wastes, usually at a comparatively late date, often during the last two or three centuries. Typical of these were places like Dunkirk in Kent and Lye Waste in Worcestershire. Lye Waste, like Coalville, is a recent settlement. It originated on the uncultivated waste of Lye village, and is said to have been "settled by a numerous body of men, who acquired a right of separate freehold on the passing of an enclosure act..." It consisted chiefly of nail-makers, and of cottagers employed in the local iron and coal works. Part of the settlement, Carless Green, was "noted for insurance clubs called Stewpony societies, and for an institution designed to improve the condition of the labouring classes, called the Stewpony Allotment Society." By 1870 there were at least four Dissenting chapels on Lye Waste.[3] The story of this community, with its numerous small freeholders and many Dissenters,

[1] *Imp. Gaz.*, *sub* Kimcote, Walton [Leics.]; nineteenth-century Leicestershire directories; *The National Gazetteer of Great Britain and Ireland* [1868] (hereafter cited as *Nat. Gaz.*), *sub* Kimcote, Walton [Leics.]. The Methodist and Baptist meeting places were in Walton village. The latter is still in use.

[2] Sarah E. Wise, *Coalville: the Origins and Growth of a Nineteenth Century Mining Town*, Leicester M.A. thesis (1968), 1, 3, 7, 15, 21n., 63; *Imp. Gaz.*, *sub* Coalville.

[3] Samuel Lewis, *A Topographical Dictionary of England* (1833), *sub* Lye Waste; *Nat. Gaz.*, *sub* Lye; *Imp. Gaz.*, *sub* Lye.

would well repay detailed exploration. The association between an outlying settlement, independent cottagers, rural industry, and Nonconformist propensities is characteristic of many Midland manufacturing villages like this in the early days of industrialization. It was an association that had a very long tradition behind it.

The origins of Dunkirk, in Kent, are more obscure. It has been claimed as an Anglo-Norman settlement; but there appears to be no documentary evidence for its existence in the medieval period. According to the *Imperial Gazetteer* of 1870 "the name Dunkirk was first given to it, about the middle of last century, by a body of squatters, who took free or forcible possession of the land, and who became notable for smuggling practices." This account, however, seems to date the origin of the settlement rather too late. More probably, like many other squatters' communities, it originated during the seventeenth century, when for a time the French town of Dunkirk became an English possession. At all events, by the early eighteenth century the Kentish place was sufficiently important to be regarded as a distinct 'ville' or township, and was certainly 'extra-parochial'. Situated within the old Forest of Blean, outside any parish jurisdiction, and within a few miles of the north coast of Kent, it became a notorious centre for smugglers and highwaymen. According to Hasted (1799) it was "inhabited by low persons of suspicious characters, who sheltered themselves there, this being a place exempt from the jurisdiction of either hundred or parish, as in a free port, which receives all who enter it without distinction," so that "the whole district from hence gained the name of Dunkirk."[1]

The inhabitants of Dunkirk were probably amongst those whom Wesley inveighed against as 'savages' when he preached in this area after returning from America.[2] In the early nineteenth century the 'ville' became the chief centre of a notorious sect in East Kent, led by John Nichols Tom, the self-styled Sir William Courtenay, who ultimately claimed to be the Messiah. The story of this sect has been more than once described by local historians. It came to a tragic end in 1838, when, after a series of riots and impostures, Courtenay and seven of his followers were killed by the Kentish militia in the battle of Bossenden Wood. The desperate poverty and brutality of the area revealed by these events profoundly shocked the local gentry and clergy; their ignorance of conditions in Dunkirk is itself an interesting comment on the isolation of an outcast community of this kind. In an effort to civilize the inhabitants an Anglican church and school were built about 1840, and in the following year Dunkirk

[1] Hasted, *op. cit.*, ix, 3–4; *Imp. Gaz.*, *sub* Dunkirk; *Nat. Gaz.*, *sub* Dunkirk.
[2] Cf. Richard Green, *John Wesley: Evangelist* (1905), 176. Wesley is said to have been preaching at or near Faversham, on the edge of Blean Forest. It is possible he was referring to the townsmen, but more probably to the forest inhabitants, who were notoriously lawless.

was formed into a separate parish. "The process of reclaiming the bad characters of Dunkirk began", says a recent historian, "almost as if a mission had been started in some far-off equatorial jungle, instead of in Kent."[1] In 1888, the Reverend W. J. Springett, who had by then been vicar of Dunkirk for 35 years, remarked that "the clergy had had a very uphill work in reclaiming the neighbourhood from the ignorance and immorality which were the results of a long period of neglect." By the time he wrote, however, their efforts had been "crowned with sufficient success to make Dunkirk no longer distinguishable from any other Christian and civilized neighbourhood."[2] The history of Dissenting vagaries in the area, with their strange mixture of idealism and delusion, had come to an end. There was no longer much that was shocking, or perhaps much that was interesting, about it. Even now, however, the events of those times have not passed out of local memory.

The association between Dissent and boundary settlements or extra-parochial tracts is obviously a subject that needs more extensive study than can be given to it here. It would also be profitable to explore a similar connexion with disputed boundaries in a number of provincial towns as well as rural areas. In late seventeenth-century Leicester, for example, the local justices and the corporation had a good deal of trouble with illegal conventicles in the extra-mural suburb known as the Bishop's Fee. The jurisdiction over this area had long been a matter of dispute between the town and the bishop of Lincoln (and later the county), and it was not finally resolved until the nineteenth century. In all probability there was also a connexion between these conventicles and the illicit trading and innkeeping for which the area became noted. Part of it, still known in the early nineteenth century as No Man's Land, had developed as the chief centre of Leicester's great autumnal fair.[3] An association of this kind between a disputed jurisdiction, illicit conventicles, and dubious trading activities seems to have been characteristic of a number of market towns in the seventeenth and eighteenth centuries. In many cases, probably, there was a connexion with the fraternity of travelling merchants, carriers, and factors, by whose means radical religious ideas were readily propagated. Certainly Stourbridge Fair, near Cambridge, was noted not only as a mart of national importance but as a centre of Puritan disturbance as early as Queen Elizabeth's reign.[4]

---

[1] P. G. Rogers, *Battle in Bossenden Wood*, 1961, 202.   [2] Quoted *ibid.*

[3] Helen Stocks, ed., *Records of the Borough of Leicester . . . 1603–1688* (1923), 259 *et passim*; C. J. Billson, *Medieval Leicester* (1920), 114–15; V.C.H., *Leicestershire*, IV (1958), 48, 54, 57–8, 350.

[4] Cf. Alan Everitt, *Change in the Provinces: the Seventeenth Century* (1969), 42–3. A carrier noted for disseminating religious ideas was John Brown (?1627–1685), the Covenanting martyr. He was a small farmer and carrier of Priestfield, Ayrshire, and was known as the 'Christian carrier'. He was ultimately shot by order of Claverhouse at his own door and in his wife's presence. Cf. *Dictionary of National Biography*, s.v. John Brown.

Decayed Market Towns

Yet another form of local community which was particularly prone to Dissent was the decayed market town. Such places were not absolutely distinct from the 'freeholders' parishes' or indeed from boundary settlements; for in most former markets landownership tended to be subdivided, and a number of towns had been founded on parish boundaries. Nevertheless, the proliferation of Dissent in these communities is sufficiently striking to deserve separate comment.

The decline of the smaller markets of England has been a persistent theme of provincial life since the later Middle Ages. By the early fourteenth century market rights of some sort had been granted to many hundreds of English places, probably to at least 1,500 and perhaps as many as 2,000. These markets were often particularly numerous along the main trunk routes of the time. On what is now the A6 through Leicestershire, there were at least seven market centres within 33 miles: Kegworth, Loughborough, Mountsorrel, Leicester, Great Glen, Kibworth, and Market Harborough. By the early sixteenth century, however, fewer than half the medieval markets of England had managed to survive as trading centres. In the late sixteenth and early seventeenth centuries there was a slight increase in numbers once again; but in the 1670s there were still no more than about 800 market towns and villages in the whole of England.[1] In most counties numbers dropped once again during the eighteenth century and much of the nineteenth, and by the end of Queen Victoria's reign, though no precise figures can be given, there were only about half as many active markets as in the seventeenth century. In Leicestershire, for example, the number had fallen from 13 in the 1670s to seven in the 1880s, and in Northamptonshire from 15 to nine.

The reasons for this decline lie outside the scope of this paper, but two general points may be mentioned. The decline between the fourteenth and early sixteenth centuries was no doubt chiefly due to the drastic fall in population, coupled with the fact that more markets had been founded than were economically necessary. The later decline, between the seventeenth and nineteenth centuries, was chiefly due to other causes. One of the most important was the gradual improvement of transport, which enabled the larger trading centres, such as Leicester, Maidstone, and Northampton, to attract trade away from the smaller places, such as Hallaton, Billesdon, Yalding, and Brixworth.

Though so many places declined as markets, however, they did not, as a rule, die out completely as human communities. Places like Stapleford in Leicestershire and Fawsley in Northamptonshire, it is true, had ceased to exist even as

---

[1] A. M. Everitt, 'The Marketing of Agricultural Produce', in *The Agrarian History of England and Wales*, IV, *1500–1640*, ed. Joan Thirsk, 1966, 469 and n., 472, 475–6.

villages three or four centuries before Queen Victoria's reign. But most of the old market centres of England remained considerable villages after their trading functions died out. The populous rural community, with no local squire, but a large number of independent freeholders, and an agrarian economy diversified by various local crafts and small industries, was a very characteristic feature of pre-industrial England, far more so than today, and more so than is generally recognized. Such places were certainly not confined to any one district, and in many cases they had originated as market towns during the great period of medieval expansion between the twelfth century and the fourteenth.

In Leicestershire many of the larger villages of the county – Kibworth, Arnesby, Kegworth, Hallaton, Belton, Billesdon, Shepshed, and Great Glen, for example – had once been small market towns. When they lost their trading functions, they remained sizeable rural communities, and it was probably often because of overpopulation that they were driven to develop local industries, such as framework-knitting, during the eighteenth and nineteenth centuries. In Northamptonshire the same features are apparent, and many of the lace-making and shoe-manufacturing villages of the county, like Brixworth, Finedon, and Irthlingborough, probably owed their populousness to their original status as markets. In Kent, nearly all the so-called 'villages' of the county are strictly speaking decayed market towns rather than agricultural villages: Ightham, Wrotham, Charing, Elham, Yalding, Smarden, Wingham, Westerham, Wye, Goudhurst, Chilham, Lenham, and many others – all come within this category.[1] There had been nearly 100 medieval market centres in Kent, but by Queen Victoria's reign more than 70 of these had relapsed into village status.

In the nineteenth century, parishes of this kind were almost invariably amongst the chief strongholds of rural Dissent. Virtually all had Nonconformist chapels of some kind, most had more than one, and many had three or four. In Kent, for instance, there were 33 rural communities with two or more Nonconformist chapels in 1851, and of these nine or ten had once been markets, and five others, like Cranbrook and Sevenoaks, still existed as small country towns.[2] With its long Puritan traditions and its five Dissenting chapels, Cran-

[1] Information on former market status has been based on miscellaneous local histories, and county histories such as Hasted, *op. cit.*; John Nichols, *The History and Antiquities of the County of Leicester* (1795–1815); John Bridges, *The History and Antiquities of Northamptonshire*, ed. P. Whalley (1791); George Baker, *The History and Antiquities of the County of Northampton* (1822–41); *Imp. Gaz.*; S. Lewis, *A Topographical Dictionary of England*, 4 vols. (1833); *Royal Commission on Market Rights and Tolls* (1889), I, 108–31 (list of market grants, 1199–1483); V.C.H., *Northants.*, *passim*.

[2] The nine or ten were: Brabourne, Goudhurst, Headcorn, Lamberhurst, Lydd, Marden, Wingham, Westwell, Chevening, and probably Brenchley; the five: Cranbrook, Sevenoaks, Bromley, Ashford, and Tenterden.

brook is a particularly interesting example. For centuries it had been the chief market and clothing town of the Weald; but in 1833 Lewis had to record that "within the last fifty years its trading importance has been almost annihilated."[1] Nevertheless, Cranbrook remained the local mecca of Dissent, Baptists, Independents, Unitarians, Wesleyans, and Huntingtonians all being represented in the little town of probably about 2,500 inhabitants.[2] The Baptist traditions of the place were so strong that in 1725 a font for total immersion was installed in the parish church, in order to encourage the conversion of Baptists to Anglicanism. The Huntingtonians had originated in Cranbrook and were locally numerous in the Weald. They had been founded by one William Huntington, a native of the parish and something of a local prophet, who at his death in 1813 had published 81 separate religious works, most of which went through several editions.[3]

In Northamptonshire and Leicestershire much the same situation obtained as in Kent. In the former county, where there were 51 rural communities with more than one chapel, four still existed as small towns, 11 were certainly decayed markets, and possibly six others came within the same category.[4] In Leicestershire, where 62 rural parishes had two chapels or more in 1851, five were still small towns, 12 had certainly once been markets, and perhaps four others.[5] In the latter county many towns or former towns had at least three chapels, amongst them Kegworth, Kibworth, Bottesford, Shepshed, Whitwick, Mountsorrel, Market Bosworth, Wymeswold, and Castle Donington. Between 46 and 57 of the 146 rural parishes where Dissent was strongest in these three counties, therefore, either were or had once been market towns, and this proportion was not untypical of other English counties.

For Lindsey the present writer has not tracked down former markets with the same thoroughness as elsewhere, so that strictly comparable figures cannot be given. There were in fact many more rural parishes with two or more chapels in this area, so that the proportion that had once been, or still were, small

---

[1] Lewis, *op. cit.*, *sub* Cranbrook.

[2] The population of the parish in 1831 was 3,844, but much of this was not resident in the town but in the subsidiary hamlets of this very large parish.

[3] Lewis, *loc. cit.*

[4] The four were: Daventry, Brackley, Oundle, and Towcester; the eleven: Brigstock, Culworth, Great Brington, Helpston, Irthlingborough, Rothwell, Byfield, Long Buckby, Finedon, Kings Cliffe, and Rushden; the six: West Haddon, Burton Latimer, King's Sutton, Raunds, Earls Barton, and Middleton Cheney.

[5] The five were: Lutterworth, Market Harborough, Ashby de la Zouch, Melton Mowbray, and Hinckley; the 12: Belton, Billesdon, Castle Donington, Kegworth, Barrow upon Soar, Bottesford, Kibworth, Market Bosworth, Mountsorrel, Shepshed, Whitwick, and Wymeswold; the four: Walton-by-Kimcote, Tilton, Great Easton, and Syston. It is arguable that one or two of the 12 should be regarded as still extant markets (e.g., Mountsorrel).

markets may well have been somewhat lower. Nevertheless, in Lindsey too Nonconformity burgeoned with remarkable fecundity in such places. In Caistor, Alford, Spilsby, Barrow, and Market Rasen, for instance, there were at least three Dissenting chapels in 1851; in Crowle, Barton, Donington, Epworth, and Tattershall there were four; in Brigg there were five, and in Haxey, as already remarked, as many as 12. Even the tiny community of Market Stainton, lost in the depths of the Lincolnshire Wolds, its market-place silent and deserted for centuries and its population shrunk to a mere 140 persons, was not without its Methodist chapel in 1851.

Quite why places of this kind encouraged Nonconformity to such an extent is a question which only intensive examination of the history and social structure of each community would answer. Though no doubt every case was in some respects peculiar, however, certain general features may be distinguished. The original grant of market status, and often of burgage rights, had attracted outsiders to these communities, increased their population, and conferred a measure of freedom upon their inhabitants. When the burghal functions died out, the tenurial structure tended to survive; independent freeholders were still numerous, the communities remained populous, and no doubt a certain tradition of independence continued to shape their history. When they reverted to village status, therefore, they remained villages with a difference. Most of them retained their annual fairs till the nineteenth century, even where they had lost their markets as early as the fourteenth. Many continued to exist as small centres of retail trade, and expanded as local centres once again with the rise of the 'village shop' in the later eighteenth century.[1] With the general increase of population about this time and the consequent growth of the livestock trade, some were also able, temporarily, to revive their markets by the establishment of monthly cattle sales.[2] From the later seventeenth century onwards most of them, particularly in Leicestershire and Northamptonshire, developed crafts or industries of some kind, such as framework-knitting, lacemaking, cloth-weaving, and shoe-manufacturing, probably often to employ an increasing surplus of population.[3] For these and other reasons the inhabitants of decayed markets were better able than most country-folk to preserve a certain

---

[1] The village shop, as an economic institution, is perhaps rarely found before 1750. From the last quarter of the eighteenth century it rapidly becomes a widespread phenomenon. The subject would well repay detailed investigation.

[2] 'Monthly markets' for the sale of livestock were a predominantly late-eighteenth and early-nineteenth century institution. They are an important indication of the rapid growth of the livestock trade at this time, concomitant with the growth of population and particularly the expansion of cities. By the 1810s they seem to have been held in some hundreds of market towns, both large and small. Many are recorded in Lewis, *op. cit.*

[3] See pp. 34 sqq.

independence of the squirearchy, and to please themselves, to some extent, in matters of religious opinion.

In some cases historical influences of a far older kind may well have played a part in the Nonconformist propensities of decayed markets.[1] Not a few, particularly in Kent, had existed as regional centres of some sort for centuries before the grant of a market by the crown. In a sense they had probably always been traditional meeting places, and for geographical and historical reasons they continued to fulfil this function, to a certain extent, long after their markets declined. Some, for instance, like Minster-in-Thanet, had been amongst the earliest centres of Christian worship in the county, becoming parent churches for a widespread region, and often continuing, till the eighteenth or nineteenth centuries, to exert a certain local dominance over their daughter communities.[2] Others had existed as centres of heathen cults well before the advent of Christianity, like Wye in Kent, originally the head of one of the lathes of the county, whose name means 'sacred place' or 'idol'. Others again were tribal meeting places or centres of ancient *regiones*, like Oundle in Northamptonshire, 'place of the Undalas' (an obscure Anglo-Saxon tribe), or Eastry in Kent, the centre of the *gē* or district of the 'eastern dwellers'. It is not without interest that the nomenclature of very many of the 96 medieval markets of Kent belongs to the earliest period of English settlement, their place-names frequently ending in *-ingas* or *-ham*. It is also remarkable that these parishes were often much larger in area than those surrounding them. Elham, Cudham, Cobham, and Wye, for example, are several times the size of the average downland parish in their area. They were all very early original centres of settlement, there is reason to think, from which the smaller parishes around them were probably colonized as secondary communities. Of course there was no direct connexion between these early historical characteristics and the development of Dissent in places of this kind. But the early influences continued to shape the social and agrarian structure of each community, as a relatively populous village and a meeting place, and it was this structure that seems to have encouraged the development of Nonconformity.

One other interesting characteristic of many decayed markets where Dissent

---

[1] Lollard connexions might be worth exploring in this context. Mr James Crompton tells me that Kibworth and Mountsorrel were amongst the most prominent centres of Lollardy in Leicestershire. Both were markets, and both became important strongholds of Nonconformity in later centuries.

[2] The parishes of St John's-in-Thanet, St Lawrence-in-Thanet, and St Peter-in-Thanet do not seem to have become completely independent of Minster till the eighteenth century. In Hasted's time the manor of Minster still 'claimed paramount' over the greater part of them (*op. cit.*, d, 332, 359, 380). Hasted dates the independence of the three churches, however, from the dissolution of Minster Abbey in 30 Henry VIII (*ibid.*, 352, 375, 404).

tended to flourish remains to be mentioned. Quite a number of them, such as Elham in Kent and Culworth in Northamptonshire, were situated at the junction of ancient tracks or droveways, and there may well have been a direct connexion in these cases between their Nonconformity and the rise of the wayfaring and droving fraternity. At Culworth the prehistoric Welsh Road (from the north-west) and Banbury Lane (from the south-west) meet in the market-place. By the sixteenth century Culworth had lost its market, but it still retained its fairs, and these probably increased with the growth of the Welsh cattle trade to Northamptonshire, utilizing these routes, in the seventeenth and eighteenth centuries. Certainly at this time Culworth became a local centre of Nonconformity. The chapels of the Baptists and the Moravian Brethren still exist in the village, adjoining the Welsh Road, and within a bowshot of the medieval market cross. It is neither untypical nor without significance that in the eighteenth century Culworth also became notorious as a centre of highwaymen – the infamous Culworth Gang.[1] The growth of the travelling fraternity and the tradition of freedom in communities of this type probably go some way to explain both historical developments.

Industrial Villages

Another and better-known form of rural community where Dissent flourished in Victorian times was the rural craft centre or industrial village. Such places cannot be rigidly distinguished from the types of local society hitherto discussed. Many were in any case parishes where property was 'subdivided' or 'much subdivided'. Many had once been markets, more, certainly, than are yet recognized as such, and many more in counties like Leicestershire and Northamptonshire than the present writer once realized. Nevertheless industrial villages are a sufficiently distinct species to be discussed on their own. In the two Midland counties under review, they were particularly numerous in the nineteenth century. There were many places, like Somerby in east Leicestershire, with an industrial character at that time, which now appear wholly rural. As might be expected, places of this kind were relatively uncommon in the less industrialized counties of Lindsey and Kent, though a thorough scrutiny of directories and censuses would probably reveal many unsuspected examples.

In Leicestershire the present writer has examined 61 rural parishes where industries provided one of the chief sources of livelihood, and in Northamptonshire 42. This is certainly not a complete list. An exhaustive study, parish by parish, would bring many others to light; but these are enough to demonstrate

[1] H. A. Evans, *Highways and Byways in Oxford and the Cotswolds* (1905), 100–1.

the propensity of this type of community to Dissent.[1] In these 103 parishes there were nearly 200 Nonconformist chapels of various denominations, or to be precise 182. In Leicestershire there were, on the average, at least two chapels to every industrial village. In only seven of the 61 was there no organized Dissent; in 18 parishes there were three or four chapels and in one (Shepshed) there were five. In Northamptonshire the tendency was less striking, but there also it was evident. All but seven of the 42 parishes had Dissenting chapels of some kind; 19 had at least two, and seven had three or four.[2]

The types of Dissent represented are of some interest. The denomination of 70 per cent of the 182 chapels has been discovered.[3] In industrial parishes of this kind, with an exceptionally numerous working class, it might be expected that essentially proletarian sects like the Primitive Methodists would be most numerous. But this was not the case: in both counties Primitive Methodists were the smallest of the four principal denominations in industrial villages, with only four chapels in the 42 Northamptonshire villages and 13 in the 61 places in Leicestershire. The Independents and Wesleyans, on the other hand, who usually comprised a rather more prosperous element in the local community in these counties, were far more numerous, with 22 chapels in parishes of this kind in Northamptonshire and 43 in Leicestershire.[4]

These facts seem to suggest that the chief force behind the growth of Dissent in the industrial villages of the east Midlands may not have been the expansion of the working class so much as the emergence of a lower middle class. Quite who composed this expanding element in village society it would be hazardous to guess without detailed examination of chapel records. Was it the master craftsman, or the workshop-owner, or the shopkeeper, or the 'aristocracy of labour', or the prospering smallholder, or some other category? Most probably it was a combination of several of these groups, and of others. Whatever the answer, if the surmise of an expanding lower middle class is correct, it suggests an important field for further research in the development of rural societies during this period.

[1] Dr L. A. Parker, in his account of the Leicestershire hosiery industry (V.C.H., *Leics.*, III), prints (20–23) a valuable table of villages where framework-knitting is recorded. Altogether evidence of framework-knitting occurs in 118 villages and hamlets in the eighteenth century. In many of these we do not know how many frames were involved; but Felkin's return of 1844, summarized by Dr Parker, shows that in 57 villages and towns in the county there were more than 50 stocking-frames, and in 40 there were more than 100. The latter, at any rate, must be regarded as industrial villages.

[2] See Appendix, Table V. The information on which the table is based has been drawn principally from *Imp. Gaz.*, mid-nineteenth century directories, and V.C.H., *Leics.*, III, 'Industries'.

[3] See Appendix, Table VI.

[4] These figures relate to the 127 chapels whose denomination is known (70 per cent of the total of 182). If the denomination of the remaining 55 chapels were known, the totals would of course be different, but there is no reason to think that the *proportions* would be altered.

Quite as interesting as the type of Dissent was the variety of industries repre-sented in these villages. In this respect there were obvious differences between the two counties.[1] In Leicestershire by far the most important rural industry was framework-knitting. By the 1860s the stocking-frame was well established in at least 45 of the 61 villages. Quarrying and coalmining also employed large numbers of people in the north-west of the county, where they were to be found in at least 13 parishes. At the little market centre of Mountsorrel, for instance, upwards of 600 men and boys were said to be employed in the granite quarries behind the town in 1870.[2] No other industry in the county appears to have ap-proached these in general importance; but locally, in villages here and there, the following industries provided a means of livelihood: brickmaking (Osga-thorpe and Sutton Cheney); earthenware (Billesdon); carriage and livery lace (Lubenham); blast furnaces (Nevill Holt); glovemaking (Quorndon); and lime-burning (Waltham on the Wolds). In many Leicestershire villages more than one industry was established. At Ibstock, for instance, coalmining was found alongside brickmaking; at Somerby brickmaking alongside framework-knitting; at Wymeswold framework-knitting with lacemaking; at Syston framework-knitting with malting and gypsum-working; at Shepshed frame-work-knitting with quarrying, glovemaking, and needlemaking; at Measham silk-weaving with smallware-making, brewing, and the manufacture of steam boilers; and at Kegworth framework-knitting with embroidery, basket-making, malting, and brewing.

The stocking-frame had first been introduced into Leicestershire in the mid-seventeenth century, at Hinckley. The social and economic conditions behind its rapid spread during the eighteenth and early nineteenth centuries have never been fully explored for the county as a whole. In some villages, like Walton and Kimcote, it seems to have been deliberately introduced, at a time of rising population, to relieve unemployment and reduce the burden on the poor rates.[3] This may well have been a widespread motive for its introduction else-where in the county, for example at Wigston Magna and in Leicester itself. Frequently knitting seems to have been combined with farmwork, for in its origins it was essentially a cottage and family employment, occupying men, women, and children too in certain stages of the work. Probably for this reason framework-knitting was especially widespread in the old wood-pasture region of west Leicestershire, where many villages have remained semi-industrial until the present day. In the early or mid-nineteenth century, however, it was also

---

[1] See Appendix, Table VII.   [2] *Imp. Gaz.*, *sub* Mountsorrel.

[3] *Ex inf.* Rev. R. A. Cowling, based on a study of local poor law records. Dr L. A. Parker's article on the hosiery industry (V.C.H., *Leics.*, III, 8) suggests that the overseers of the poor often apprenticed paupers in their charge to the master-knitters in Leicestershire.

well established in eastern and southern Leicestershire, for example at Frisby, Kibworth, Walton, Billesdon, and Somerby, where nowadays one would not suspect any former industry.

Was the stocking-frame introduced into these parishes as a result of parliamentary enclosure and the conversion of arable to pasture, or were older and more subtle causes at work? The history of communities like these needs the intensive examination which Professor Hoskins has devoted to Wigston Magna, in *The Midland Peasant*, before a very positive general answer can be given. It may be observed, however, that many of these places, like Billesdon, Kegworth, and Kibworth, were decayed, but still populous, market centres;[1] whilst others resembled the large 'open' villages of Warwickshire described by Dr J. M. Martin in *The Agricultural History Review* in 1967.[2] What we really need to know is more about the occupational structure of such places in the crucial period from 1750 to 1800. In Leicestershire, however, we do not have the excellent militia lists of counties like Northamptonshire and Buckinghamshire, which enable us to make a general analysis of rural occupations at this time.

In Northamptonshire no single industry was so prominent as framework-knitting in Leicestershire. The three that took its place were shoemaking (in 16 of the 42 villages), lacemaking (in at least 12), and quarrying (in 10).[3] The principal shoemaking area in the county was in the east, around Kettering and Wellingborough, in such villages as Raunds, Rushden, Finedon, and Irthlingborough. At this date shoemaking was more dispersed than today, however, and it also obtained in villages like Long Buckby and Green's Norton, in west Northamptonshire.

Lacemaking was probably much more widespread in Northamptonshire than the above figure suggests. Essentially it was a cottage industry, chiefly undertaken by women and girls, and for these reasons the censuses and contemporary gazetteers and directories rarely refer to it. All along the Buckinghamshire border it was prominent, and it also extended right up through the western half of the county, as far as Market Harborough in

---

[1] At least 11, and possibly as many as 20, were decayed markets.

[2] J. M. Martin, 'The Parliamentary Enclosure Movement and Rural Society in Warwickshire', *The Agricultural History Review*, xv, i (1967). It is interesting that in many of Dr Martin's 'open' villages land was still described as 'subdivided' or 'much subdivided' in 1860, and several of them were also decayed markets (e.g., Brailes, Napton, Brinklow, and Aston Cantlow). Probably a thorough search would show that many of the 'open' villages of the Midlands, where inhabitants were numerous and land was subdivided, were in fact decayed markets. Many of them (though not all) certainly developed as characteristic Dissenting villages, with small local industries as well as agriculture to support their inhabitants. See also p. 21, n. 1, *supra*.

[3] See Appendix, Table VII. For fuller lists of Northamptonshire shoemaking villages see *Shoemakers in Northamptonshire, 1762–1911: a Statistical Survey*, Northampton Historical Series, No. 6, ed. V. A. Hatley, 1971.

Leicestershire.[1] Later in the century the craft of lacemaking was killed off by the Nottingham machine-made lace industry; but it was still an important feature of the Northamptonshire economy in the 1860s. Small towns like Towcester, Brackley, and Higham Ferrers, and former markets like Brixworth and Irthlingborough, were still lacemaking centres. In villages like Moulton (near Brixworth) and Hanslope (just in Buckinghamshire) there were lace-schools. In some of these the children were entered at the age of five years and when arrived at that of eleven or twelve were said to be able to support themselves by their labours.[2]

The semi-industrial nature of many Northamptonshire villages and those of neighbouring parishes in Buckinghamshire, has its origins some way back in their history, before the nineteenth century. The Northamptonshire Militia List of 1777 and the Buckinghamshire *Posse Comitatus* of 1798 prove this beyond any doubt. In Table IX the occupational structure of 17 of these parishes is given, and these indicate the existence of several quite distinct types of rural community in this area. By the late eighteenth century, it is clear, the economy of many of these parishes was no longer based entirely on agriculture, but on a wide variety of local crafts, small industries, and distributive trades. Even in the ten most completely agricultural villages in the Northamptonshire sample, a quarter of the population was engaged in non-agricultural pursuits. In Ravenstone, Kingsthorpe, and Hanslope the non-agricultural proportion was about one-third; in Hardingstone it was 40 per cent; in Moulton 43 per cent, and in Spratton more than 60 per cent. These are figures which may be compared with 90 to 95 per cent in an essentially urban community like Northampton.

At the other end of the scale is the curious exception of Stoke Goldington. Though one of the most populous of the 17 parishes, only 7 per cent of its inhabitants appear to have been engaged in anything but farmwork. Possibly some of the many 'labourers' in the parish in fact worked in the local ironstone quarries; perhaps many of the women, girls, and boys worked at lacemaking. Whatever the explanation, it would be interesting to know just what was happening in this seemingly anomalous community on the Northamptonshire–Buckinghamshire border at the end of the eighteenth century.

Hanslope is a classic example of a decayed market. By this date, probably, almost the whole of its market place had been filled in with houses, shops, and cottages. With an area of 5,290 acres, the parish was much the largest in the

---

[1] M. D. Eaton, *Victorian Market Harborough: the Structure and Functions of a Nineteenth-Century Market Town*, Leicester M.A. thesis (1969), 45, 46.

[2] Lewis, *op. cit.*, *sub* Hanslope; *Imp. Gaz.*, *sub* Moulton, Hanslope. The Moulton schools were still functioning in the 1860s.

area, and, with probably more than 1,000 inhabitants, decidedly the most populous. Though its market functions were extinct, it had either remained or was becoming once again a local craft and trade centre, with five grocers, five victuallers, six lace-dealers, six tailors, seven bakers, 10 butchers, 15 shoe-makers, 29 other craftsmen, and an apothecary.

None of the other parishes where crafts or industries were prominent, how-ever, can apparently be explained, like Hanslope, as decayed markets. The economy of Hardingstone was no doubt influenced by its proximity to North-ampton; but Spratton and Moulton were completely independent villages. They were not in former forest country and they had never been markets. And yet their occupations were more diverse and more 'industrial' than any of the other 15 parishes. They seem, in fact, to be clear examples of the 'open' villages of the Midlands described by Dr J. W. Martin.[1] Unlike the ten 'agricultural' parishes they had no single resident squire, but many small farmers employing only a small labour force, possibly only their own sons and kinsmen. In the mid-nineteenth century the land in these parishes was still 'much subdivided'; their economy was still semi-industrial; and they were prominent centres of Non-conformity. Nowadays, unlike many similar villages in Leicestershire and eastern Northamptonshire, they have reverted once again to a largely rural or residential character.

Despite the variety of occupations in these counties, there is little evidence that any particular industry proved more conducive to Dissent than others. "Scratch a cordwainer and find a Dissenter" is an oft-repeated gibe at the religious propensities of the shoemaking fraternity. But though the shoemakers' predilection for Nonconformity was remarkable, it is doubtful if it was more striking than that of lacemakers, framework-knitters, or many other kinds of village craftsman. In the 46 villages in the two counties where framework-knitting was established there were 94 chapels, in the 16 shoemaking villages 32 chapels, and in the 14 lacemaking villages 26: the proportion is virtually iden-tical for all three industries. Only in the 16 quarrying villages, where there were 23 chapels, was it noticeably lower; in Northamptonshire particularly so, with only eight chapels in ten quarry villages.[2] Quite clearly a more important fac-tor in the proliferation of Dissent than the type of industry was the social struc-ture of the local community in question. There was no special or unique con-nexion between cordwaining and Dissent in the nineteenth century, any more than there was between clothmaking and Dissent in the seventeenth. The signi-ficant factor was rather the social and economic structure of the local commu-nity itself.

Somewhat similar in character to these industrial villages were the new rail-

[1] *Loc. cit.*   [2] See Appendix, Table VIII.

head and canal settlements of the nineteenth century. In these, too, Dissent usually established a firm foothold. Sometimes, as Dr D. A. Iredale has found at Barnton on the Trent and Mersey Canal in Cheshire, virtually the whole community became Dissenters: in this, as in many cases, Methodists.[1] Without detailed local examination it would not be possible to say what proportion of the inhabitants was Nonconformist in similar settlements to Barnton in the counties here studied; but their Dissenting propensities are not difficult to establish. In Leicestershire, for example, there were Nonconformist chapels at Rearsby, a small river port on the Wreake, and at Foxton, an old village which developed a new wharfside settlement near its flight of locks on the Grand Junction Canal. Further south, on the same canal, at Stoke Bruerne in North-amptonshire, the Wesleyan chapel of 1879 stands alongside the wharf, the warehouse, the Boat Inn, and the cottages of the canal community. The establishment of chapels in settlements of this kind was sometimes a matter of deliberate policy on the part of the sect concerned. It was undertaken with a view to 'civilizing' their inhabitants and curbing their lawless propensities.

In Lincolnshire several of the villages bordering the Trent developed into busy little riverside ports at this time, and usually these were strongly Nonconformist. Owston Ferry or West Ferry is a case in point. The parish of Owston in the Isle of Axholme stretched for nine miles alongside the Trent, from the boundary with Nottinghamshire to the parish of Althorpe. By the 1860s a brewery, a ropewalk, a boat-building yard, a brick and tile yard, an oil-cake mill, several corn mills, and packing and sailcloth manufactories had sprung up at West Ferry. There were three Dissenting chapels in this little river-port, for Wesleyans, Primitive Methodists, and United Free Methodists, and there was also a Wesleyan school.[2]

In Kent there were few comparable village ports of this kind, but there were several railhead settlements with a somewhat similar history. One was Paddock Wood in the Weald, an entirely new village which sprang up after the building of the first railway in the county, from Redhill to Dover, at its junction with the branch line to Maidstone. Paddocks or Parrocks was an old manorial estate which had passed through the hands of a succession of landed families in Kent, but there had apparently never been a village or hamlet on the site. The new railhead was astutely placed, however, and it rapidly developed into a sizeable community with the expansion of orchards and hop-gardens in the area. By 1860, with a population of nearly 900, the village was large enough to be formed into a separate chapelry, and there seem to have been at least two

---

[1] D. A. Iredale, *Canal Settlement: a Study of the Origin and Growth of the Canal Settlement at Barnton in Cheshire between 1775 and 1845*, Leicester Ph.D. thesis (1966), 207 sqq., 'Religion', *et passim*.

[2] *Imp. Gaz.*, *sub* Owston [Lincs.].

Dissenting groups established within it.[1] Further west on the same railway line, a similar development took place at Edenbridge. This was not a new village, but an early daughter settlement of Westerham, probably founded soon after the Conquest. With an area of 5,300 acres and a scattered agricultural population in 1801 of more than 900, Edenbridge was a typical Wealden parish, similar in extent and character to its neighbours Leigh, Penshurst, Cowden, and Chiddingstone. With the coming of the railway, however, it developed a new role as the farming and commercial centre of this district. Its population trebled between 1801 and 1921, whilst that of its neighbours remained static or by 1900 began to decline. By the 1860s Edenbridge had acquired a weekly corn market and a monthly cattle market, and it had become the centre of a new and at that time important hop-growing district. Apart from the ancient church of St Peter and St Paul, there were Independent and Baptist chapels in the village and these were sufficiently powerful to establish their own British school.[2]

The growth of Edenbridge and Paddock Wood was conditioned not only by the railway but by the local development of intensive farming, principally in fruit and hops. Though in Kent, as elsewhere, most rural parishes remained static in population or declined during the latter half of the nineteenth century, there were a number of agricultural parishes in the county, like Edenbridge and Paddock Wood, where population continued to expand because of the need for a large labour force, especially in orchards and hop-gardens.[3] In a sense these villages were the Kentish equivalent of the 'industrial' villages of Leicestershire and Northamptonshire: much of the local surplus of population did not need to migrate to the towns, but was able to find employment in the surrounding countryside, though in this case not in workshops but on farms. Agriculture was much the most important local industry, and farm labourers were more numerous in Kent than in any other county of comparable size.

Intensive farming communities of this kind, in Kent and probably also in Lincolnshire, seem to have encouraged Dissent in much the same way as the industrial villages of the east Midlands. At East Peckham, for instance, a populous parish in the heart of the Wealden fruit and hop area, whose inhabitants increased by more than 1,000 between 1801 (1,327) and 1861 (2,341), there

---

[1] Hasted, op. cit., v, 286–8; Imp. Gaz., sub Paddock Wood; local observation.

[2] V.C.H., Kent, III, 368; Imp. Gaz., sub Edenbridge; Nat. Gaz., sub Edenbridge.

[3] It should be stressed, however, that fruit and hops were not so universal a feature of Kentish farming as is commonly supposed. Over most of the county they were of little importance. In the 1860s they appear to have accounted for less than a tenth of the cultivated area, and pasture farming was far more extensive. Apart from Lincolnshire, the county had much the largest acreage of permanent pasture of any lowland county (280,000 acres). In relation to its area it also had the largest sheep population in Britain (731,000), though in absolute terms both Devon and Lincolnshire (769,000 and 1,088,000 respectively) surpassed it. Nat. Gaz., XII, Appendix, 4.

were at least two Dissenting chapels by the latter date, for Wesleyans and Cal-vinistic Methodists. In this case the population was also partially employed in tanning and seed-crushing mills, and this may have helped to account for Non-conformist tendencies.[1] The economy of the neighbouring parishes of Marden and Brenchley, however, where there was a similar rise in population and a comparable tendency to Dissent, seems to have been entirely agricultural in its basis. Here there was no kind of industry; apart from a few shopkeepers and craftsmen, the inhabitants must have been employed in the orchards and hop-fields, and many of them were certainly Nonconformists. Baptists and Wes-leyans both had chapels in Brenchley, and Wesleyans and Independents in Marden. At Newington, situated amongst orchards and hop-grounds near Sittingbourne, and at Ash-by-Wingham, a few miles inland from Sandwich, very similar conditions obtained. In each parish the land was intensively farmed, a large labour force was employed, the population rose gradually throughout the nineteenth century, and Methodism or Congregationalism flourished.[2]

Other Forms of Community

In the Midlands there were a number of Dissenting parishes where the condi-tions hitherto described did not obtain, or at least probably did not fully ac-count for the presence of Nonconformity. The significant feature about many of these remaining parishes is that they did not conform to the normal Midland form of a single nucleated settlement, but consisted of a number of dispersed hamlets or subsidiary townships.[3] In area, too, they were often large by Mid-land standards, where as a rule the typical parish extended to no more than 1,500 or 2,000 acres. Whether in all cases the Nonconformist chapels of the 1860s were to be found in the outlying hamlets of these localities, away from the parish church, only detailed topographical study of each place in question would prove. In many cases known to the present writer, however, they cer-tainly were.

---

[1] *Imp. Gaz.*, *sub* Peckham, East; *Nat. Gaz.*, *sub* Peckham, East. East Peckham is interesting from another point of view. The present agricultural/industrial village is 2½ miles from the parent parish church of St Michael, isolated on its hill top. The historical evolution of the economy of the parish would form an interesting subject for detailed study.

[2] V.C.H., *Kent*, III, 360, 362, 364. See also the relevant entries for Brenchley and Marden in *Imp. Gaz.* and *Nat. Gaz.*; for Ash-by-Wingham in *Imp. Gaz.* (as Ash-next-Sandwich) and *Nat. Gaz.* (as Ash-near-Sandwich); for Newington in *Imp. Gaz.*, *Nat. Gaz.*, and Lewis, *op. cit.* Marden, Newington, Ash, and possibly Brenchley, it is interesting to note, all come within the category of decayed markets. The growth of population between 1801 and 1851 was less marked in Ash-by-Wingham and Marden, amounting to about 500 or 600, or 35 per cent; it remained static thereafter.

[3] The following paragraphs are based on the relevant parish entries in *Imp. Gaz.* and *Nat. Gaz.* and where possible on local fieldwork in each county.

In Lincolnshire the parish of Bottesford, where there were two Nonconformist groups, covered more than 5,000 acres and comprised five distinct townships. Laughton, also with two chapels, was a parish of nearly 4,000 acres, including 1,000 acres of sandy common and the subsidiary hamlet of Wildsworth. Corringham, where there were also two chapels, covered more than 6,000 acres and comprised four subsidiary hamlets. Broughton, with two chapels, extended to nearly 7,000 acres and included the subsidiary township of Castlethorpe as well as the hamlets of Manby and Gokewell. There were a number of other parishes of this kind in Lindsey whose history would repay further exploration. Several of those mentioned, such as Corringham and Broughton, appear to have been places of very early primary settlement, like the larger downland parishes of Kent referred to on an earlier page, and this may have partly accounted for their peculiarities.

In Leicestershire the parish of Nailstone covered nearly 4,000 acres and comprised the subsidiary settlements of Normanton le Heath and Barton in the Beans, in each of which there was a Nonconformist meeting-place. Church Langton, with at least one Dissenting group, consisted of four distinct townships and covered more than 4,000 acres. Prestwold, where there were two chapels, comprised three hamlets and covered nearly 5,000 acres. Rothley, with three chapels, covered 5,500 acres and included five separate townships within its borders. Tilton and Breedon, with two chapels each, were smaller parishes – each a little over 3,000 acres – but these also comprised several distinct townships. Once again a number of the Leicestershire instances, for example Breedon and Tilton, were places of early primary settlement.

A somewhat similar pattern was repeated in Northamptonshire, though there the parishes concerned were for the most part smaller. In Potterspury parish there was an Independent chapel at Yardley Gobion, an outlying village which had no church of its own till 1864. In Weedon Lois the Baptist chapel was at Weston, and in Blakesley at Woodend, both of which were subsidiary hamlets with no Anglican church. The parish of Pattishall comprised as many as six outlying hamlets – Astcote, Dalscote, Eastcote, Foster's Booth, Foxley, and Catchem's End – and contained two Nonconformist meeting-places, for Baptists and Primitive Methodists. In King's Sutton there were also two chapels, and this parish comprised the hamlet of Walton and parts of Charlton, Astrop, and Purston, as well as the church-village of King's Sutton itself. These Northamptonshire parishes were all in the wooded part of the county towards the Buckinghamshire and Oxfordshire borders. Their settlement pattern and that of this district as a whole was a mixture of nucleated Midland villages and scattered forest hamlets not unlike those of the Weald of Kent. And, as in the Weald, it is interesting to note that most of the Nonconformist chapels of the area belonged to the Old Dissenting persuasions of Baptists and Independents. Compared with Lindsey or east Leicestershire they were comparatively little affected by the new Dissent of Methodism.

In all three Midland counties there were a number of parishes where most of the property was in a single landlord's hands and neither local industries nor scattered forms of settlement seem to explain the presence of Dissent. In most of these places it is noteworthy that the landlord concerned did not live in the parish itself but was either an absentee or else resident in a neighbouring village. As a consequence, despite the concentration of land in a single hand, there was a certain degree of freedom for the local village folk from the immediate eye of their landlord. There were a number of Dissenting chapels in east Leicestershire, for example, in the estate parishes of the Duke of Rutland and the Earl of Dysart: at Saltby, Sproxton, Sewstern, Hose, Plungar, and Redmile, to mention a few by name.[1] These places were well away from the seats of the two landed families concerned, which were at Belvoir and Buckminster. In the estate parishes of the squirearchy, by contrast, as distinct from those of titled magnates of this importance, Dissenting chapels seem to have been noticeably rarer. Sometimes, it is clear, manorial control was more vigilant on the smaller landed estates covering only one or two parishes than on the far-flung domains of Midland dukes and earls.

The type of Dissent represented in parishes of this kind was almost invariably Wesleyan or Primitive Methodist. No doubt this was partly because most of the large landed estates of Leicestershire and Lindsey were in areas like the Leicestershire Wolds, where there seems to have been little Dissent of any kind before the late eighteenth century. There may well, however, have been other causes at work. In some cases the local landlord himself had at one time favoured Methodism, as at Raithby by Spilsby, where in 1779 a chapel for John Wesley and his followers had been fitted up in the office-wing of Raithby Hall.[2] There can be no doubt that a more detailed acquaintance with the local history of similar parishes would bring other examples than Raithby to light. The rigid class distinction between Anglicans and Dissenters which became the commonplace of nineteenth-century literature, after the development of Anglo-Catholicism and the rise of the public schools, was certainly not universal in the eighteenth century. At the time of the Evangelical Awakening there was more interchange between church and chapel than is commonly supposed. A large proportion of the subscribers to the Congregationalist Philip Doddridge's writings in the 1740s and 1750s were squires, peers, peeresses, bishops, dons, and Anglican clergy.

[1] Sewstern was strictly a chapelry of Buckminster, but it is a separate village.

[2] N. Pevsner and J. Harris, *The Buildings of England: Lincolnshire* (1964), 337. Another example is Cardiphonia chapel at Milsted, Kent, built for the Bible Christians by the Drawbridge family.

The spread of rural Dissent in those Leicestershire estate parishes where the landlord was non-resident makes one wonder how far the growth of absenteeism generally in the late eighteenth and early nineteenth centuries facilitated the remarkable increase of Nonconformity at this time. Others have noted a similar correlation between absentee parsons and the spread of Dissent in Yorkshire, Cornwall, and Devon.[1] So far as the counties under review are concerned, absenteeism, whether of squire or parson, does not seem to have been the principal factor because, as we have seen, Dissent was in any case far more prolific outside estate parishes, in the freeholders' communities. Yet the effects of absenteeism may well have been significant in areas like east Leicestershire and Lindsey. The growth of absenteeism at this time must not be exaggerated; but with the development of more rapid coaching services and the amalgamation of estates through intermarriage, many manor houses sank to the level of farmhouses, and the London season was able to attract more and more families away from their estates and from the local season in the county town. In Lincolnshire, Nottinghamshire, and Northamptonshire for a variety of reasons the local county town was gradually ceasing by the early nineteenth century to focus the life of the county community in quite the same way as hitherto.[2]

When the future Viscount Torrington perambulated the Midlands in the 1780s he deplored ,"in my old style, the desertion of the country by the gentlemen and good yeomanry. An hundred years ago, every village afforded two good gentlemen's houses; and within these sixty years, the hall or the court still remained. These were the supporters of the poor and of their rights, and their wives were the Lady Bountifuls of the parish... But since the increase of luxury and turnpike roads, and that all gentlemen have the gout and all ladies the bile, it has been found necessary to fly to the bath and to sea-bathing for relief ... whilst the old mansion being deserted and no longer the seat of hospitality ... is left to tumble down; and with it the strength and glory, and I may add the religion of the country. For whilst decent and pious families therein resided, the minister attended to his double Sunday duties... But the families being gone, no longer are these duties continued; and the divine himself, from lack of company, pays a pitiful stipend to a hackney curate (who rides over half the country on a Sunday) and retires to London or to Bath."[3] Torrington's views, it is true, were coloured by sentiment and exaggeration. The conditions he de-

---

[1] R. Currie, 'A Micro-Theory of Methodist Growth', *Proceedings of the Wesley Historical Society*, XXXVI (1967), 69 and n.

[2] Of Nottingham Dr Church remarks that by 1814 "many of the town-dwelling gentry had quit their mansions for the country, while the frequent and regular gatherings of the 'polite society' at the Nottingham 'assemblies' had been discontinued." (R. A. Church, *Economic and Social Change in a Midland Town: Victorian Nottingham, 1815–1900* (1966), 14.) For Lincoln see Sir Francis Hill, *Georgian Lincoln* (1966), chapter XI *et passim*.

[3] C. B. Andrews, ed., *The Torrington Diaries...*, II (1935), 238. I owe this reference to Joan Simon.

scribed were far from universal and in some respects they proved only a passing phase. By Trollope's time, after all, the scandalous Stanhopes of the Barchester Close were already looking pretty old-fashioned. Yet Torrington's words were not without a certain foundation in fact. And it is not difficult to envisage why Nonconformity should have spread in the kind of parishes he described, where neither squire nor parson cared twopence about their more humble parishioners.

Conclusions

It is clear, then, that rural Dissent in the mid-nineteenth century was associated with a wide spectrum of settlement types. What were the common elements, if any, between these varied forms of local community? At the risk of considerable oversimplification they may be said to have been threefold. In the first place they were almost all marked by an unusual degree of freedom: freedom either in the sense of comprising many small freeholders, self-employed craftsmen and tradesmen, or some similarly independent group of inhabitants; or else in the sense of being situated well away from the nearest parish church and in many cases far from any manor-house. Amongst the former places were the freeholders' parishes, the decayed markets, the industrial villages, and many 'open' villages with a large labour force in areas of intensive farming, such as Brenchley and Ash-by-Wingham in Kent. Amongst the latter were the subsidiary or outlying hamlets of primary centres of settlement; the boundary communities and places that sprang up on extra-parochial tracts, like Lye Waste and Dunkirk; and many squatters' communities or new settlements connected with canals or railways, such as Barnton and Paddock Wood. In so far as Dissent was associated with subsidiary settlements and outlying hamlets, it follows that it was especially prolific, generally speaking, in areas of scattered settlement like the Weald, the Pennines, Cornwall, and Wales. But by 1851 it was by no means confined to areas where settlement was dispersed, for it was at least equally powerful in nucleated villages and decayed markets wherever these contained a sizeable number of independent freeholders, craftsmen, or tradesmen.

The second characteristic common to many Dissenting communities is at first sight more surprising. This was the tendency for Nonconformity to develop principally either in communities of *very early* origin or in areas of *very late* settlement. This tendency is not universally apparent, but it was often a striking feature in the pattern of rural Dissent. On the one hand many of the wood-pasture areas where Nonconformity flourished, such as the Weald, were regions of large parishes and predominantly late, post-Conquest colonization. Still later were the squatters' communities of the sixteenth and seventeenth

44

centuries with which Dissent was associated, and the new industrial villages of the eighteenth and nineteenth. On the other hand many of the decayed markets and 'open villages' where Dissent proliferated seem to have originated as communal settlements of 'the folk' during the earliest phases of the Anglo-Saxon invasions. Certainly many strongly Nonconformist settlements in Northamptonshire and Kent, such as Oundle and Wye, were places that had originated at a very early period, sometimes as centres of an Anglo-Saxon 'tribe' or *regio*.

There is nothing really mysterious in the association of Dissent with very early and very late settlements, or its relative absence from those of intermediate date. The social and economic structure of the former places was often inherently favourable to Nonconformity. Certainly in Kent and probably in Leicestershire, Northamptonshire, and Lindsey many early places had originated as *communal* settlements and throughout their history they remained large and populous parishes comprising a numerous body of independent freeholders. In some sense many of them have always remained local meeting-places, and for this reason too they tended to become the focal points of religious life: first perhaps (as at Wye) for the worship of a heathen deity, then as minster churches of the Anglo-Saxon kingdoms, and finally (at a much later date) as centres of Protestant Nonconformity. The settlements of intermediate date, by contrast, in Kent at least, tended to be small manorial parishes originating in the generations immediately preceding the Conquest and founded by a single individual or family. Their churches were in origin often manorial chapels established by the local lord and intimately associated with his hall. And throughout their history, speaking generally, they have tended to remain the preserve of an exclusive squirearchy, and to have resisted the incursions of Nonconformity.

A third general characteristic of rural Dissent, following in part from the foregoing point, may be more tentatively advanced. In three at least of the four counties under review there was a marked tendency for the Old Dissent of the Baptist and Congregationalist communions to prevail in forest and wood-pasture areas, with their large parishes and scattered forms of settlement: whilst the New Dissent of Methodism tended to predominate, sometimes to a remarkable extent, in the generally smaller and more arable parishes of the limestone and lias belts. This contrast was especially evident in Leicestershire and Kent. Before the rise of the New Dissent, rural Nonconformity in Kent was almost confined to the Weald and chartlands; in Leicestershire it was chiefly found in the predominantly wood-pasture areas in the western half of the county. By 1851 Nonconformity had spread to many chalk parishes in Kent and to the lias and limestone settlements of east Leicestershire, where in almost every case it was some form of Methodism, and not the Baptist or Congregationalist faith, that took root.

In Lincolnshire, where there was very little wood-pasture but much chalk and limestone country, the Old Dissent had always been weak and Methodism, as has been seen, was by 1851 uncommonly strongly entrenched. The same kind of development has been observed by Dr David Hey in the arable belt of magnesian limestone parishes in south Yorkshire, where Congregationalism hardly ever established itself successfully. In Northamptonshire the pattern was not so simple. This county was in some respects less sharply divided into distinct agrarian regions than Leicestershire and Kent, and the old forest areas of Rockingham and Whittlewood had in any case undergone more radical transformation than west Leicestershire or the Weald. Nevertheless, about two-thirds of the traditionally Nonconformist parishes in this heartland of the Old Dissent were to be found in the woodland areas of Rockingham, Salcey, and Whittlewood.

In concluding this section it must be emphasized that these generalizations should not be pressed too far. Even in the four counties here studied they were not universally valid – the following section shows some marked peculiarities in the case of Northamptonshire, for instance – and detailed examination of other shires may well bring to light a good deal of variation from what appears to be the norm.

III FOUR COUNTY PORTRAITS

HITHERTO we have been considering chiefly the points of similarity between the four counties concerned in this study. Each region, however, was also possessed of a certain character of its own, and in each the pattern of rural Dissent was to some extent shaped by the local history and social structure of the shire. Within the limits of this paper, only some of the salient local peculiarities can be mentioned, and to grasp these it is first desirable to say a little more about religious allegiance generally in mid-Victorian England.

Judged by the number of 'sittings' recorded in the census of 1851, 44 per cent of the church-going population as a whole at this time were Dissenters, and 56 per cent Anglicans.[1] The census figures are probably in some areas misleading, particularly in the eastern counties where there were many large parish churches serving small and dwindling populations. In Norfolk and Suffolk particularly the number of 'sittings' probably exaggerates the strength of Anglicanism by a considerable margin. It is quite possible that Dissenters

[1] See Appendix, Table II.

may have formed half, or nearly half, the population in these two counties. Nevertheless, the census figures are not without significance, and when all allowance is made they indicate a number of striking regional differences in the pattern of Dissent.

At a first glance, the analysis of religious allegiance in Table II[1] seems to suggest two principal and not unfamiliar tendencies in this pattern. In the first place Nonconformity appears to have been more powerful in the north than the south. In the whole of the north-east, from Derbyshire and Nottinghamshire up to the Scottish border, Dissenters apparently comprised more than half the communicant population, and in Durham and Northumberland as much as 60 per cent of it.[2] In the counties south of the Thames, by contrast, they generally formed little more than one-third of the population. Secondly, Dissenters often appear to have been more strongly represented in industrial than in agricultural counties. The ten counties with the highest percentage of Anglicans – about two-thirds or more of the church-going population – were all predominantly agrarian, including Herefordshire, Rutland, Oxfordshire, Shropshire, Westmorland, Dorset, Hampshire, Sussex, and Kent.[3] In counties with a good deal of industry, like Yorkshire, Derbyshire, Nottinghamshire, and Durham, by contrast, they formed less than half the population.

These overall tendencies certainly cannot be ignored; but the more closely they are examined, the more unsatisfactory they appear as generalizations. To some extent the disparities between different counties were merely due to the fact that Anglican churches tended, for historical reasons, to be more numerous in the south than the far north. West of the Pennines, moreover, in contrast with the east, Dissenters nowhere formed as much as half the population, and in Westmorland the proportion was exceptionally small (34 per cent). In Staffordshire and Lancashire, two of the most industrial counties in England, the Nonconformist proportion was markedly lower (42 per cent and 46 per cent) than in agrarian counties like Huntingdonshire, Cambridgeshire, and Bedfordshire (48 to 52 per cent).[4] In the predominantly agricultural North and

---

[1] See Appendix, Table II.

[2] In the Teesdale area of County Durham Nonconformist 'sittings' were more than twice those of Anglicans. The figures were: Anglicans, 3,185; Nonconformists, 6,570 (Independents, 1,065; Baptists, 540; Quakers 333; Wesleyans 2,619; Primitive Methodists, 1,958; Unitarians 55). Northumberland was clearly much influenced by its proximity to Scotland, and was the only county with a considerable number of Presbyterians at this date (29,928 sittings).

[3] Professor Pevsner remarks on the paucity of Nonconformist chapels in Hampshire, and points out that the early ones are "very small and modest. . ."—N. Pevsner and David Lloyd, *The Buildings of England: Hampshire and the Isle of Wight* (1967), 48n.

[4] In the St Ives area of Huntingdonshire, Dissenters appear to have far outnumbered Anglicans. There were more than 8,000 'sittings' in the Nonconformist chapels of the area and only 5,000 in the churches of the Establishment.

East Ridings the proportion of Dissenters, though lower than in the West Riding, was still remarkably high by national standards, amounting to more than half the church-going population. Finally, we must not forget that absolute numbers may be as significant as percentages in assessing the strength of Dissent. And these show that of the 13 counties with more than 100,000 chapel sittings in 1851, eight were in the south and only five in the north, whilst four were predominantly industrial and seven or eight at this date predominantly agrarian: Kent, Somerset, Norfolk, Devon, Gloucestershire, Lincolnshire, Cheshire, and Cornwall.

These words of caution are not intended to suggest that there was no causal connexion between forms of regional society and forms of religious allegiance. But they do suggest that a microscopic examination of the society of each county, of the social structure of each local community within the county, and of the Dissenting sects and chapels within each community is necessary if the pattern of rural Nonconformity in England is to be explained. The facts gleaned for the present study contribute, of course, only a partial solution to this problem; but each of the four counties examined yields something by way of an answer.

Lindsey

With nearly 50 per cent of its population Dissenters, Lincolnshire was decidedly the most strongly Nonconformist of the four counties. Its population was not much more than half that of Kent; but its Dissenters outnumbered those of Kent by more than 30,000. The remarkable feature about Nonconformity in Lincolnshire was the extraordinary strength of Methodism and the weakness of the older Dissenting sects. The Independents and Baptists formed only 9 per cent of the church-going population compared with 17 per cent in Kent, 23 per cent in Leicestershire, and 28 per cent in Northamptonshire. Methodists, by contrast – that is, all the varied Methodist groups together – comprised nearly 40 per cent of the population compared with 21 per cent in Leicestershire and only 14 or 15 per cent in Northamptonshire and Kent.[1] The power of Methodism in this part of England was not confined to Lincolnshire, but reached northwards through Yorkshire and Durham, westwards into Nottinghamshire and Derbyshire, and southwards into East Anglia.[2] It is a curious fact – was it conceivably anything more than a curiosity? – that, apart from Celtic Cornwall, the most strongly Methodist area of England coincided almost exactly with the counties of the Danelaw. Was there some peculiarity inherent in their society that proved conducive to this kind of Dissent?

[1] See Appendix, Table X.

[2] See Appendix, Table II. The vast majority of Dissenters in these counties, as recorded in the table, were Methodists.

The other remarkable feature about Lincolnshire was the extraordinary number of parishes where all the land was in the hands of a single magnate.[1] In Leicestershire there were 20 such parishes (out of 250); in Northamptonshire 29 (out of 282); in Kent there were none whatever (out of 340). In Lindsey, by contrast, there were no fewer than 73 out of 374. In other words in 20 per cent of Lindsey parishes all the land was owned by a single magnate, as compared with 10 per cent in Northamptonshire, 8 per cent in Leicestershire, and *nil* in Kent. In these landlords' parishes Dissent was virtually never able to establish itself, in fact in only two cases. In the Lindsey parishes where land was in a few hands, Nonconformity was also conspicuous by its absence, noticeably more so than in Leicestershire or Northamptonshire. In other words Lindsey was a county where the contrast between the Anglican 'estate' parishes and the Dissenting 'freeholders'' parishes was exceptionally sharp. On the one hand there seems to have been a remarkable number of overweening magnates in the county, like the Earl of Yarborough, who had acquired control over all the land in their own and neighbouring parishes, and virtually never suffered Nonconformity to appear. On the other hand there were the numerous freeholders' parishes where Dissent not only found a footing but flourished with unusual fecundity.[2] This point is reinforced by the contrast between Lindsey and Kent. In both counties there were approximately 100 freeholders' parishes where the land was 'much subdivided': but whereas in the former shire there were two or more chapels in 64 of these parishes, in the latter there were two or more in only 26.[3] And this despite the fact that in Kent such parishes were normally larger and more populous than in Lindsey. Altogether there were two or more chapels in nearly 30 per cent of the rural parishes of Lindsey (110 out of 374) and in many there were three, four, five, or even more: whereas in Kent there was more than one in only 10 per cent of such parishes, and there were hardly ever more than two.[4]

Leicestershire

Leicestershire is interesting for different reasons. As a county it was only a little less strongly Nonconformist than Lincolnshire (47 per cent of sittings); but the Old and New Dissent were more evenly balanced (Methodists 21 per cent, Baptists 15 per cent, Independents 8 per cent), and there was a marked geographical cleavage in religious allegiance.[5] The chief stronghold of Methodism was in the uplands of north and east Leicestershire: the lias and limestone country and the valleys bordering Lincolnshire, Rutland, and east North-

[1] See Appendix, Table XI.   [2] See Appendix, Tables XII and XIII.
[3] Compare Tables XII and XXVII in the Appendix.
[4] Compare Tables XIII and XXVIII in the Appendix.   [5] See Appendix, Table X.

49

SHL
WITHDRAWN

amptonshire. Before the advent of Methodism there was practically no Nonconformity in this half of the county. According to John Evans's list of Dissenting Congregations in George I's reign (in Dr Williams's Library, London), there were only four such groups in east Leicestershire out of 37 in the county as a whole.[1] The stronghold of the more traditional Dissenting sects, by contrast (Baptists and Independents), was in the old wood-pasture region to the west and south of the county, towards Staffordshire, Warwickshire, and west Northamptonshire. Dissent had in fact a very long and interesting history behind it in this part of the county. A number of chapels still in existence today can trace their ancestry back to the seventeenth century. Villages like Arnesby and Kibworth and towns like Ashby de la Zouch were Nonconformist centres of more than local importance long before the days of Wesley and Whitefield.

The contrast between Anglican estate parishes and Dissenting freeholders' parishes was certainly less striking in Leicestershire than elsewhere. There were fewer parishes without any Nonconformists than in the other three counties,[2] and many more estate parishes than in Lindsey or Kent where Dissent managed to establish itself (27 per cent of all estate parishes, compared with 18 per cent in Lindsey, and 14 per cent in Kent). It is also significant that there were noticeably more parishes in Leicestershire with three or more chapels than elsewhere. More than two-fifths of the 'much subdivided' rural parishes of the county had three or more chapels, compared with 30 per cent in Lindsey, 16 per cent in Northamptonshire, and only 8 per cent in Kent.[3]

There can be little doubt that one of the most important factors behind these peculiarities in Leicestershire was the large number of industrial villages in the county. Leicestershire was certainly the most industrialized of the four counties but there was only one large town in the shire and no old incorporated borough apart from Leicester itself. Its industries, especially framework-knitting, lace-making, and quarrying, were to a considerable extent rural, and perhaps its most characteristic form of society in the nineteenth century was the semi-industrial village. Such communities were often remarkably populous and almost always very prone to Dissent. They were among the places where there were three or four Nonconformist chapels in 1851. Altogether there were 22 rural communities in Leicestershire with three chapels, and 11 with four or five.[4]

---

[1] Cf. also R. H. Evans, 'Nonconformists in Leicestershire in 1669', *Trans. of the Leics. Arch. Soc.*, xxv (1949), p. 110.

[2] See Appendix, Table XIV. There were 114 parishes out of 250 in Leicestershire where there was no Dissenting chapel (45 per cent). This compares with 200 out of 374 in Lindsey (53 per cent); 163 out of 282 in Northamptonshire (58 per cent); and 208 out of 340 in Kent (61 per cent). (See Tables XII, XIV, XVI, XXVII.)

[3] See Appendix, Table XIV.   [4] See Appendix, Table XV.

Perhaps almost as important was the fact that there were comparatively few large landed estates in Leicestershire, except in the north-east of the county.[1] In strong contrast with its neighbour Northamptonshire, and to some extent Lindsey, it was not a shire of great country houses. Nor does one often find in Leicestershire those splendid manorial pews and elaborate monumental pedigrees which are still so common a feature of the parish churches of Kent. A not untypical Leicestershire parish, like Kimcote, had no squire in the nineteenth century, nor had it had one for several generations. Its society was composed instead of a small number of independent farmers and graziers, a few shopkeepers and craftsmen, and a large number of framework-knitters.[2] Not all Leicestershire parishes of course resembled Kimcote, but this was a very characteristic form of village society in the county in the eighteenth and nineteenth centuries.

Northamptonshire

In Northamptonshire the pattern was different from that of either Lindsey or Leicestershire. Anglicans were rather more numerous (56 per cent of 'sittings') and Nonconformists less so (44 per cent) than in the two former shires. This generalization, however, conceals what is in fact the most interesting feature of the county, namely the remarkable strength of the old Dissenting bodies. Both Baptists and Independents formed a larger proportion of the population in Northamptonshire than in any of the other three counties – thrice as large as in Lincolnshire – and taken in conjunction they were twice as numerous as all the branches of Methodism put together.[3] Of the old Dissenting bodies, the Baptists were also very powerful in the two adjoining counties of Bedfordshire and Huntingdonshire, and both Baptists and Independents in nearby Cambridgeshire.[4] There were probably few counties where the Old Dissent as a whole was more powerful or more deeply entrenched than in Northamptonshire.

The reasons for the strength of the Old Dissent in the county cannot be fully explored here. They would indeed require a good deal more research than the present writer has been able to give them. But two points of interest may be made. In the first place several of the most influential figures in Baptist and Congregationalist circles during the preceding century had been Northamptonshire pastors, in particular Philip Doddridge, the two John Rylands, and William Carey. Carey's tenure of office in the county had been brief, but as a

---

[1] The great estates of the Duke of Rutland and Earl of Dysart, for example, were centred in the north-east. The latter owned more than 8,000 acres in Leicestershire and the former more than 30,000 acres.

[2] *Imp. Gaz., sub* Kimcote; nineteenth-century Leicestershire directories; *ex inf.* Rev. R. A. Cowling.

[3] See Appendix, Table X.   [4] *Imp. Gaz., sub* these three counties.

son of Northamptonshire and founder of the Baptist Missionary Society, he became something of a local hero. The influence of the John Rylands, father and son, had been fundamental in the Evangelical Awakening among Baptists, and their reign had been based for more than thirty years (1759–93) upon College Street Chapel in Northampton. Equally important, at an earlier stage in the Awakening, was the influence of the Congregationalist Philip Doddridge, not only through his chapel and academy in Northampton itself but also by means of his preaching-tours and above all his writings and hymns.

In the second place the strength of the Old Dissent in Northamptonshire went back far beyond the eighteenth century. It derived much from the fierce Puritanism of the county town and many of the country gentry at the time of the Civil War. It owed something to the Northampton 'Prophesyings' and the classical organization of the county set on foot during the reign of Queen Elizabeth.[1] Its ancestry was directly traceable of course to Robert Browne, the founder of Congregationalism, who later conformed and held the living of Thorpe Achurch from 1591 to 1631, dying in Northampton gaol, probably in 1633.[2] Ultimately there was almost certainly a direct connexion between the Old Dissenting groups of the county and the survival of local Lollard traditions.

So far as landownership was concerned, the most striking feature of Victorian Northamptonshire was the remarkable proportion of estate parishes. In two-thirds of the parishes of Northamptonshire all the land was concentrated in the hands of a single magnate or a few large proprietors: a figure which may be compared with 59 per cent in Lindsey, 52 per cent in Leicestershire, and 36 per cent in Kent. In only 13 per cent of the parishes in the county was landed property described as 'much subdivided' in the Return of 1860, in comparison with 24 per cent in Leicestershire, 26 per cent in Lindsey, and 44 per cent in Kent.[3] There were many rural parishes in Northamptonshire, such as Marston St Lawrence with its 535 inhabitants and 122 houses (1861), where despite the size of the population all the property was in a few hands, or a single hand, and no Dissenting group succeeded in establishing itself. Many of the former market towns of the county, moreover, had by the 1860s become mere estate parishes, with all their land engrossed by a single magnate or a few wealthy proprietors: amongst them Aynho, Fawsley, Grafton Regis, Rocking-

---

[1] These remarks are based on the author's unpublished research into the history of Northampton and Northamptonshire in the sixteenth and seventeenth centuries, and into family allegiance during the Civil War period, based principally on contemporary tracts and borough records.

[2] *Dictionary of National Biography*, s.v. Robert Browne.

[3] See Appendix, Table XI. Owing to the wide variation in parish-size in Kent, the figures for this county have been re-worked on an acreage basis: see Table XXIV. These give the percentages mentioned for Kent in the text above.

ham, Naseby, Brigstock, Culworth, Helpston, and Chipping Warden.[1] There was no real parallel to this situation in the other counties, where, as already remarked, landownership in the old market towns tended to remain minutely subdivided long after trading functions had disappeared.

Some of the principal reasons for these peculiarities in the structure of land-ownership in Northamptonshire are not far to seek. They were due to the over-whelming power of the landed phalanx in the county. In 1797 the county was said to be "completely under the control of about a dozen peers" in matters of politics. In the early nineteenth century there were said to be more peers resi-dent in Northamptonshire than in any shire of comparable size.[2] Certainly there were (and still are) many more palatial family mansions than in any similar county. It is beyond the scope of this paper to trace the process by which these families and their estates came into being, but a few figures relating to the estates and rent rolls of several Northamptonshire peers in the nineteenth century may be cited.[3]

With an estate of 8,000 acres in the county and an income of £26,000 a year, Lord Lilford's property, centred on Lilford Hall near Oundle, was a compara-tively modest one by local standards, though he also owned 7,500 acres in other parts of England. With much the same landed income, the Marquess of Northampton owned nearly 10,000 acres in Northamptonshire, chiefly around his seat at Castle Ashby, and a further 5,000 acres not many miles away in Warwickshire. The income of Earl Spencer in the western half of the county amounted to nearly £50,000 a year, and his estates covered more than 27,000 acres, of which nearly 17,000 were in Northamptonshire and 3,400 in War-wickshire. Around Burghley House, in east Northamptonshire, the Marquess of Exeter owned nearly 25,000 acres, of which 16,000 acres were in Northamp-tonshire and 9,000 in Rutland. These estates yielded the marquess an income of almost £50,000 a year, apart from which he also owned very valuable pro-perty in London.

Even the Marquess of Exeter's estates paled into insignificance before those of the princely Duke of Buccleuch. One of the most important factors in the growth of landed estates in Northamptonshire had been the tendency to inter-marriage amongst the peerage, and no family had benefited from this com-

---

[1] *Imp. Gaz., sub* these places.

[2] E. G. Forrester, *Northamptonshire County Elections and Electioneering, 1695–1832* (1941), 5, quoting T. H. B. Oldfield, *History of the Original Constitution of Parliaments* (1797) and *The Representative History of Great Britain and Ireland* (1816), iv, 275.

[3] The following paragraphs are based on the entries in G.E.C., *The Complete Peerage. . .*, ed. Vicary Gibbs, relating to Lord Lilford, the Marquess of Northampton, Earl Spencer, the Marquess of Exeter, and the Duke of Buccleuch; *Dictionary of National Biography,* s.v. Walter Francis Scott, fifth Duke of Buccleuch.

fortable process more than the Montagu-Douglas-Scotts. By the nineteenth century they had united the fortunes and the blood of at least three dukedoms, those of Montagu, Queensberry, and Buccleuch. By the 1880s the Buccleuch estates extended to more than 460,000 acres, an area almost as great as the whole of Leicestershire or Westmorland. In terms of value, says *The Complete Peerage*, they were "by far the most considerable in the kingdom". They yielded his Grace an income of more than £217,000 a year. Most of this vast principality was in Scotland, where the duke owned a quarter of a million acres in Dumfriesshire alone. In terms of acreage the Northamptonshire property was comparatively modest, a mere matter of 18,000 acres with a further 7,000 acres in nearby Warwickshire. In fact the palace of Boughton, near Kettering, was regarded as quite one of the minor seats of the family, though its splendid gardens alone covered more than 100 acres, and the famous avenues established in the early eighteenth century by the great 'planting duke', the second Duke of Montagu, extended to more than 70 miles.

With such an estate behind him it is not surprising that the fifth Duke of Buccleuch, who succeeded at the age of 13 in 1819 and reigned for 65 years, was said to be something of a *grand seigneur*. His habits were noted for their simplicity, "and his appearance [was] rather that of an Elder of the Kirk. He always wore a dark grey cutaway coat, shepherd's plaid trousers, and a cap with a large peak, and out of doors carried a plaid over his shoulder." This homely appearance, however, could perhaps be deceptive; for according to Sir Walter Scott "he has a natural sense of his own station, which will keep him from associating with unworthy companions".[1] It is hard to imagine two worlds more completely severed than those of the Montagu-Douglas-Scotts at Boughton and the fierce, combative little chapel communities in the surrounding Northamptonshire villages.

The vigour of the Old Dissenting traditions in the Northamptonshire countryside no doubt explains why there were many more estate parishes in the shire with Nonconformist chapels than in the other three counties. Despite the widespread engrossing of the smaller freeholds of the shire by local magnates, many chapels, it seems, had been able to maintain some kind of independent existence. In Kent there were chapels in only 19 per cent of these estate parishes, in Lindsey in 23 per cent, and in Leicestershire in 26 per cent. In Northamptonshire, by contrast, they were to be found in 40 per cent of these communities where peers or gentry had acquired control over nearly all the land in the parish.[2]

Nevertheless, even in Northamptonshire it is evident that Dissent was an

---

[1] Quoted in G.E.C., *op. cit.*, II, 371n.
[2] See Appendix, Table XVII, and compare Tables XIII, XV, and XXVIII.

exception in places of this kind. In few or none of the numerous parishes in the hands of the Duke of Buccleuch or the Marquess of Exeter, it seems, was there any organized form of Nonconformity. The influence of magnates like these over local religious life was reinforced by their control over church patronage. An extraordinary number of Northamptonshire livings were in the hands of aristocrats like the Marquess of Northampton, the Duke of Grafton, the Duke of Buccleuch, the Marquess of Exeter, the Duke of Bedford, Lord Hungerford, Lord Lilford, and Earl Spencer. Many other livings in the county were in the hands of Oxford or Cambridge colleges, and in these too Nonconformity was rarely able to establish itself. It seems the Victorian dons who normally held these livings were by no means well-disposed towards Dissenters. Even where property was subdivided but the local living was in the hands of an Oxford college or a local magnate, as in the Buccleuchs' parish of Winwick, it was rare to find a Dissenting chapel.[1] Sometimes, as the vicar of Naseby naïvely revealed in the 1790s, systematic economic pressure was brought to bear on Dissenters to abandon their religious loyalties.[2]

It must be confessed that, with all their real virtues, the members of the Northamptonshire phalanx might have inhabited a different planet from the humble Dissenters around them. Their sublime outlook on the world was epitomized by Oswald Barron in his volume of *Northamptonshire Families*, published in 1906. In Barron's eyes only 19 families in the county were worthy of consideration. There must have been much heart-burning in Northamptonshire drawing-rooms on the morning when this superb volume appeared. Nor can there have been much consolation in Barron's reasons for excluding everyone else in the county. "Those who find themselves within our gates", he announced, not without a certain grandeur, "may rest assured that there at least neither wealth nor title can gain admission for those without."[3] Beneath the lofty eyes of Victorian aristocrats, however, many a Northamptonshire chapel still lived out its own half-hidden life with a good deal of vigour.

Kent

There were several peculiarities in the pattern of religious allegiance in Kent as compared with the three Midland counties. In the first place, the provision of

[1] These remarks are based on information regarding patrons in the parish entries for Northamptonshire in *Imp. Gaz.* and *Nat. Gaz.*

[2] The needy were permitted to benefit from local funds available for the poor provided they attended service in the parish church. The good vicar was pleased at the number of 'sectaries' this system had brought over to the Church of England. John Mastin, *The History and Antiquities of Naseby* (1792), 78–9.

[3] A. O. Barron, *Northamptonshire Families* (V.C.H., *Northants.*) (1906), xviii.

church sittings was much less ample than elsewhere. In Lincolnshire, Leicester-shire, and Northamptonshire about two-thirds of the population could have been accommodated in the churches and chapels of the county; in Kent the comparable figure was little more than 40 per cent.[1] Put in another way there were 750 inhabitants to every church and chapel in Kent, compared with 394 in Northamptonshire, 369 in Leicestershire, and 277 in Lindsey.[2] This pecu-liarity was probably quite a recent one in Kent and chiefly due to the relatively rapid growth of population in the late eighteenth and nineteenth centuries. In Staffordshire, where the population increased a good deal more quickly than in Kent, only 36 per cent of the population could have been accommodated in church or chapel in the 1850s. Between 1801 and 1861 the inhabitants of Kent increased by 138 per cent; a figure which may be compared with a growth of 73 per cent in Northamptonshire, 98 per cent in Lincolnshire, and 207 per cent in Staffordshire.[3]

The second peculiarity in Kent has already been alluded to: the much larger number of Anglicans than Nonconformists in the county. So far as church sittings indicate, it seems that nearly two-thirds of the population (65 per cent) were Anglicans and about one-third Dissenters.[4] These figures compare closely with those of other southern counties like Sussex, Hampshire, and Dorset;[5] but as a generalization they conceal one of the most interesting characteristics of the county, namely the remarkable diversity in religious allegiance as between its different regions. Diversity of this kind, it is true, was not peculiar to Kent. There were some striking differences, as we have seen, between east and west Leicestershire. But they seem to have been more marked in Kent than in a county like Lindsey, where in all the registration districts of the Census the number of Dissenting chapels was surprisingly similar, varying only from 68 in the Horncastle district to 88 in that of Glanford Brigg.[6]

The regional diversity in Kent comes to light if the registration districts into which the county was divided are separately analysed. These districts in some cases more or less corresponded with the ancient lathal subdivisions of the county and most of them comprised between 12 and 25 parishes. An analysis of 18 of these districts, covering nearly two-thirds of the shire, proves that the chief areas of Dissent were the cathedral cities of Canterbury and Rochester, the Thanet seaside resorts and Tunbridge Wells, the dockyard towns on the Medway, and the London suburbs. In all these areas Nonconformists num-

---

[1] See Appendix, Table XVIII.   [2] See Appendix, Table XIX.

[3] See Appendix, Table XX. The growth in Kent roughly approximated to that of England as a whole: 138 per cent compared with 126 per cent.

[4] See Appendix, Table X.   [5] See Appendix, Table II.

[6] The figures for the registration districts in Lindsey were as follows: Caistor district 83 chapels, Glanford Brigg 88, Gainsborough 77, Louth 81, Spilsby 75, Horncastle 68, Lincoln 75.

bered at least 40 per cent of the population, and in the suburbs around Greenwich as much as 46 per cent.[1]

The old cathedral cities and the watering places of Victorian England were frequently strongholds of Dissent, no doubt largely because they contained a sizeable leisured class with ample time for religious speculation. (It is a mistake to suppose that the strength of urban Dissent always lay with the trading and artisan classes.) The relatively high figure for the London suburbs is interesting in view of the fact that London generally was far less prone to Nonconformity than the provincial cities of Victorian England. Suburban Dissent was, however, essentially a phenomenon of metropolitan rather than Kentish history and cannot be examined in detail here. It must suffice to say that these parts of Kent immediately around Greenwich where Dissent was most powerful in the 1850s, had had the lowest proportion of Nonconformists in the county at the time of the Compton Census in 1676 – a mere 1 per cent. Their rise to prominence in the annals of Nonconformity in the nineteenth century was due to developments in metropolitan society and had little or no connexion with the Dissenting history of the county generally. The two movements were essentially distinct in both origin and genius.

The third peculiarity of Nonconformity in Kent was that it was there a far more urban movement than in the other three counties. In Leicestershire, Lindsey, and Northamptonshire roughly two-thirds (63 to 69 per cent) of all Nonconformist chapels were in rural parishes, and only one-third were situated in the towns. In Kent the position was reversed. Out of 500 chapels in the county only about 36 per cent were in the countryside, whereas 64 per cent were in urban areas. No doubt this was partly because the urban population was larger in Kent, in absolute terms at any rate. This cannot be the only reason for the disparity, however, for the rural population was also much larger than in Leicestershire or Northamptonshire, whereas rural chapels were actually fewer in number than in any of the other counties: a mere 178 in all, compared with 187 in Northamptonshire, 245 in Leicestershire, and 344 in Lindsey.[2]

In the rural parts of Kent, only the traditional Puritan areas around Tenterden, Cranbrook, and Maidstone showed any very marked propensity to Dissent. With 36 to 38 per cent of their population Nonconformists, they were above the average for the county as a whole, and southern England generally, though still well below that of the three Midland counties (44 to 49 per cent).

---

[1] See Appendix, Table XXI.

[2] See Appendix, Table XXII. Sixty-one per cent of the rural parishes of Kent had no dissenting chapels: a figure that compares with 58 per cent in Northamptonshire, 53 per cent in Lindsey, and 46 per cent in Leicestershire.

Elsewhere in the shire Dissenters were thinner on the ground than in almost any other part of England. Herefordshire was the most strongly Anglican region of England, with only 28 per cent of its population Dissenters; but in much of rural Kent Nonconformists were even sparser than in Herefordshire. They comprised only 22 per cent of the population in the 19 parishes of Romney Marsh, 21 per cent in the East Ashford district (25 parishes), 20 per cent in Blean district (13 parishes), and a mere 15 per cent in Bridge district (23 parishes).[1]

By and large these and other predominantly Anglican areas of rural Kent corresponded with those where Dissent had been weakest in the seventeenth century. The weakness of Nonconformity in these districts was associated with the comparative stagnation of the Old Dissenting sects within them. Generally speaking the Old Dissent was a good deal stronger in Kent than in Lindsey or east Leicestershire, accounting for 58 per cent of all Nonconformists compared with 26 per cent in Lindsey and 24 per cent in east Leicestershire, though it was not so high as in Northamptonshire (68 per cent).[2] In the more strongly Nonconformist parts of rural Kent the Old Dissenting sects accounted for a good deal more than 58 per cent of all Nonconformists: in the Cranbrook area, for example, they comprised nearly three-quarters of the total.

In the most strongly Anglican areas of Kent, by contrast, Methodists formed the predominant element in rural Dissent. In the nine districts (167 parishes) where Nonconformists numbered less than one-third of the church-going population, Methodists comprised nearly 60 per cent of all Dissenters.[3] By and large these areas coincided with the chalk downlands of the county, and it can scarcely be mere coincidence that in comparable limestone areas elsewhere in England, such as the Lincolnshire Wolds and the east Leicestershire uplands, Methodists also formed, as we have seen, by far the largest Dissenting communion. There is probably nothing mysterious in this development. It was connected with the tendency for a certain type of society and landownership to develop in these chalk and limestone districts, with comparatively small parishes and a strong squirearchy. Such areas had often proved somewhat impervious to the Old Dissent at the time of the Compton Census, and were ripe for exploitation by Methodism in the following century.

When the pattern of landownership is examined, it seems at first sight some-

---

[1] See Appendix, Table XXI.

[2] The Leicestershire figure is based on the 72 parishes and chapelries of the Billesdon and Melton districts, in which there were 6,397 Methodist 'sittings', 955 Congregationalist, 975 Baptist, and 100 others. The Old Dissenting proportion for Leicestershire as a whole was 55 per cent. Like Kent, the county was sharply divided regionally in terms of religious adherence: the stronghold of the Old Dissent was in the old wood-pasture area of west Leicestershire.

[3] See Appendix, Table XXIII.

what surprising that Nonconformists should be generally thinner on the ground in Kent than in the Midlands. If the subdivision of land tended to favour Dissent, why was it that in this county, where the ownership of land was so greatly subdivided, Nonconformity was weakest? As already remarked, the freeholders' parishes of Kent covered nearly two-thirds of the county, whereas in Leicestershire they comprised only 48 per cent of rural parishes, and in Northamptonshire a mere 33 per cent.[1]

This apparent contradiction cannot be entirely explained by the present author, and was doubtless due in part to more subtle and personal causes than are taken account of in this paper. But there can be little doubt that the spread of Nonconformity was hampered by the strength of local Anglican traditions, by the influence of the two cathedral cities and their clerics, and by the high proportion of Kentish benefices in the gift of the church itself (about 270 out of 400 or so at the end of the eighteenth century).[2] Yet a more detailed analysis of the structure of landownership shows that in Kent, too, property patterns exerted a striking influence on the distribution of Nonconformity.

Underlying the local variety in religious allegiance in the county, in fact, were remarkable regional differences in the structure of landownership. In the Weald and similar forest tracts, freeholders' parishes[3] comprised in the 1850s as much as 81 per cent of all parishes in the area. In the chartlands – the greensand countryside bordering the Weald to the north – the comparable figure was only 46 per cent. In the foothills to the north of the downs, it was no more than 39 per cent, and on the chalk downlands themselves a mere 30 per cent.[4] In other words, though there were few parishes in Kent, if any, where all the land was concentrated in a single hand, as in the Midlands, in at least half the county the concentration of land in the hands of local gentry was as striking as it was anywhere in England. Unlike Lindsey, east Leicestershire, and Northamptonshire, Kent was not a county dominated by the vast estates of titled magnates like the Earls of Yarborough and Dysart, or the Dukes of Rutland and Buccleuch. But much of it was, and for centuries had been, the preserve of an indigenous squirearchy as powerful locally and apparently quite as inimical to Dissent as the aristocracy of the Midlands.

The sharp geographical division of the county into areas of 'estate parishes' and 'freeholders' parishes' closely corresponded, in general, to the ancient,

[1] See Appendix, Table XXIV. As already explained, it has been necessary to base the figure for Kent on acreage rather than the number of parishes, owing to the much wider variation in parish sizes than in the Midlands.

[2] This figure is based principally on the information regarding patronage in each parish entry in Edward Hasted, *The History and Topographical Survey of the County of Kent*, 2nd edn (1797–1801).

[3] i.e., those where the land was 'subdivided' or 'much subdivided'.

[4] See Appendix, Table XXV; cf. also Table XXVI.

basic divisions of Kent into downland and Weald. The local forms and procli-
vities of society in each region were still shaped by the original differences of
settlement pattern and social structure in these areas. With its large parishes
and late settlement forms, the Weald was still predominantly an area of small
freeholders. In a few parishes, like Horsmonden, these freeholds had by the
1850s been amalgamated into sizeable estates; but in four parishes out of five
the land still remained 'much subdivided', and Nonconformity was noticeably
more powerful than in the rest of Kent or in southern England generally. One
interesting symptom of the strength of the old freeholding class in the Weald
was the continuing use of the word 'yeoman'. In Northamptonshire the term
had virtually died out by the 1750s. In the Weald it survived till well into the
nineteenth century. It was used as late as the year 1853 on the tombstone of
Thomas King in the churchyard of Capel, near Tonbridge.

The downlands and chartlands of Kent, by contrast, were areas of smaller
parishes and in general earlier settlement.[1] In the 1850s they were still dominated by numerous little parks and manor houses, just as they had been in the
sixteenth and seventeenth centuries. Even today one of the most characteristic
features of downland scenery is the lonely parish church, with its attendant
manor house – now often a mere farm – and with hardly another building in
sight. Most of these churches originated as manorial chapels, and there is still a
strong sense of manorial dominion in a church like that of the Hart-Dykes at
Lullingstone, the Pemberton-Leighs at Frinsted, or the Granville-Wheelers at
Otterden. The family pews of the squirearchy and the numerous dynastic
monuments recording the pedigrees and achievements of their ancestors are
still striking features of many Kentish churches.

There can be little doubt in fact that the weakness of rural Nonconformity in
much of Kent was largely due to the remarkable strength of the old squirearchy
of the county in these downland and chartland areas. Honywoods and Derings,
Tokes and Twysdens, Oxindens and Knatchbulls, Streatfeilds and Robertses,
Austens, Gibbons, and Polhills: these and many similar Kentish dynasties still
exerted in the first half of the nineteenth century the same autocratic influence
as in the days of Charles I. In a sense, more than ever united by ties of marriage
in a single great county cousinage, they were yet more powerful. There was
nothing quite like their far-spreading yet intensely local clans in the Victorian
Midlands. Though virtually unknown outside the county, within it they were

---

[1] The general movement of settlement in Kent was in a southerly direction, from the downlands on
to the chartlands, and from there into the Weald. Most of the earliest place-names in the county are on
the downs or in areas adjacent to them, though there are, of course, exceptions to these generalizations.
The strength of the squirearchy in the chartlands has, in many cases, a different origin. These areas
included extensive tracts of poor terrain in which parks were established in the late medieval and
Tudor periods, and many rising gentry families established themselves.

like petty princes. Wherever they predominated Nonconformists rarely numbered more than a quarter of the village population, and in most parishes there were few or none. In more than 60 per cent of the rural parishes of Kent there was no organized Dissent of any kind.[1]

There were, however, a number of downland parishes in Kent where Dissent obtained a firm foothold by the nineteenth century. These are interesting because they were for the most part untypical of downland settlements in point of both size and social structure. The parish of Meopham, for example, covered nearly 5,000 acres, that of Cudham nearly 6,000, Elham 6,598, and Wye 7,348: whereas the average downland parish comprised less than 1,600 acres. Most of these large and strongly Nonconformist parishes on the downs belonged to the earliest phase of settlement in the area, and many of them had at some time in their history (usually during the thirteenth century) developed into market towns. For reasons which cannot be explored here they were places which never came to be dominated by the downland squirearchy, but appear to have remained the preserve of small, independent freeholders throughout their history. The history of each of them would well repay detailed examination from this point of view.

One final feature of the county of Kent remains to be mentioned. As already remarked, none of the other shires showed so marked a proclivity for the more local or eccentric forms of sect. In Leicestershire, Northamptonshire, and Lincolnshire, all but about 2 per cent of the Dissenting population (270,000 out of 276,000) belonged to the mainstream of Nonconformist denominations: Baptists, Methodists, Independents, Quakers, and Unitarians. In Kent nearly a tenth of all Dissenters (10,000 out of 104,000) belonged to such unusual denominations as the Latter-day Saints, Catholic and Apostolic Church, Plymouth Brethren, Huntingtonians, Bible Christians, Courtenayites, Jezreelites, and French Protestants. Typical of the local sects were the Huntingtonians, who were numerous around Cranbrook, where their founder William Huntington had been born in 1745; the Courtenayites, or followers of John Nichols Tom, of whom small numbers still lingered on in the 1860s (and later) around Faversham and Canterbury;[2] and, later in the century, the Jezreelites, a strange messianic body in the Chatham and Gillingham area.[3] More orthodox

---

[1] See Appendix, Table XXVII; cf. also Table XXVIII. The exact figure was 61 per cent. This compares with 58 per cent in Northamptonshire, 53 per cent in Lindsey, and 45 per cent in Leicestershire. A comparison of parishes where property was 'subdivided' as distinct from 'much subdivided', in each of the four counties, is instructive in this connexion. It is remarkable that these 'marginal' parishes were much less favourable to Dissent in Kent than elsewhere. In Lindsey, Leicestershire, and Northamptonshire only 12 to 22 per cent of them contained no Dissenting chapel; in Kent 52 per cent were without any organized form of Nonconformity.

[2] Cf. J. A. Owen, ed., *Annals of a Fishing Village* (1892), 65–7.

[3] The story of the Jezreelites has been told in P. G. Rogers, *The Sixth Trumpeter* (1963).

were the Bible Christians, a West Country sect who had more than three thousand adherents in Kent, but none at all in the Midland counties.

To explain this predilection for eccentricity in Kentish Dissent is beyond the scope of this paper; but in all probability it was not an entirely new development. The work of Dr Nuttall seems to suggest that there was a certain streak of oddity in the early Nonconformist history of the county too. Most of the Baptist churches of the seventeenth century, for example, were Arminian and not Calvinistic in character.[1] The excitability of a certain type of Kentish temperament was a local characteristic often commented upon by contemporaries, and it evidently played a part in the stranger vagaries of religious life in the county.

IV CONCLUSION: THE GENIUS OF THE CHAPEL COMMUNITY

THE mixture of similarity and diversity between the four counties may serve to remind us of the limitations of the present study. Certainly it must not be supposed that the types of community here represented were the only ones with which Dissent was associated in other parts of England. Elsewhere the pattern described in this paper was undoubtedly echoed, but probably nowhere was it precisely repeated in all its details. In the north-western counties, for example, where the parish structure was different and where there were many more wholly new settlements with which Dissent was associated – canal ports, mining villages, factory villages, and the like – the pattern was probably in some essential respects of a different kind. It may also have differed, one suspects, in parts of East Anglia, where a common form of rural community seems to have been the dual-settlement parish, divided between a 'church-end' and a 'chapel-end', the former probably the original settlement, the latter a later subsidiary hamlet chiefly composed of poorer cottages, often sited round a small green.

Neither must it be supposed that 'nonconformity' was a homogeneous movement united by common ties of class and creed. Within the limits of this study we have necessarily been concerned with Dissent as a whole, and only passing reference has been made to the remarkable diversity within its ranks. Yet it should not be forgotten that the differences between the various sects were in many ways as important as the resemblances. To take an extreme instance, there was little or nothing in common between the Unitarians and the Plymouth Brethren apart from their antagonism to Anglicanism. This antago-

---

[1] G. F. Nuttall, 'Dissenting Churches in Kent before 1700', *Journal of Ecclesiastical History*, xiv (1963), 181, 185.

nism never brought them in any conscious sense together and it is very unlikely that they would have stood together on any particular issue. They differed completely in their essential creed, their ideas of church order, their pietistic ideals, their political convictions, and their social composition. In their inflexible Trinitarianism the Brethren, like many sects at this time, would have associated themselves more readily with the established church than with the Unitarians. Even within a single movement, like Methodism, there were distinctions in origin, in religious conviction, and in social class between the Wesleyans, the Primitive Methodists, and the Countess of Huntingdon's Connexion. The very frequency with which Dissenting feuds led to the foundation of new sects shows how deep were the latent divisions between them. Many denominations had consciously separated themselves as much from the errors of their fellow Dissenters as from those of the established church. And almost equally striking, in many cases, were the differences within a single denomination at different periods in its history. One has only to compare the little brick boxes built by Congregationalists in the back streets of towns like Deal or Ashby de la Zouch in the eighteenth and early nineteenth centuries with the grandiose suburban churches erected in the 1870s and '80s, to realize the social and economic transformation that might occur within a single communion during this period.

For these reasons verbal labels like 'Radical Nonconformity', 'the Dissenting Interest', and 'the Nonconformist Conscience' can be as misleading as they are enlightening. In reality there was no such unanimity amongst Dissenters as phrases like these imply. In particular it is misleading to identify Nonconformity, *tout court*, with political Radicalism. Some sects were essentially Radical; but others were as militantly conservative in their social teaching as they were in their basic theology. The mixture of independence and conservatism may be an irritating phenomenon to those who like tidy theories and neat historical labels, but like so many awkward facts of history, it may be made to open up an important train of thought.

Nevertheless, there was a certain essential kinship of mind between many Dissenting denominations, and for this reason their unprecedented expansion in the century or so from about 1760 to 1860 calls for some comment. What occasioned this expansion, in particular (so far as the present paper is concerned) in rural communities? How can the appeal of the New Dissent during this period of unparalleled change be explained? In what did its essential genius consist? This is not the place for an extended answer to these questions, which might well occupy several lengthy volumes. Yet a few tentative and admittedly subjective impressions, based in part on a general acquaintance with the literature and hymnology of the period, may perhaps be offered.

No doubt one of the underlying reasons for the rapid growth of Dissenting societies in the countryside was the expansion of the rural population generally and its increasing geographical mobility. As country people plucked up their roots, and migrated increasingly from village to village, or settled in expanding numbers in the old market towns with their new industries, they must have felt more of a need for the intense fellowship of the chapel community. Severed from friends and family, their membership of the chapel gave them a title to new friendships, and to the support and intimacy of a new home. The peculiar genius of their own 'connexion' was something familar in an otherwise alien environment. Narrow, quarrelsome, and culturally impoverished though these Dissenting communities may have been, they provided a certain sense of safety and affection in an unfamiliar and uncertain world.

One of the most obvious evidences for this craving for the intense fellowship of chapel life was the fact that so many local Nonconformist groups originated as 'cottage meetings', that is as informal societies gathered on Sundays and weekday evenings around the hearth of one of their members. This kind of origin lent from the outset a certain domesticity to the Dissenting chapel, which was obviously lacking in the parish church. In many cases these meetings resulted in the establishment of permanent chapels, for the ultimate aim of forming a fully-fledged religious society was normally the motive behind them. Where the population was sparse or poor, however, or where the sect in question was exceptionally exclusive, these meetings probably continued for many years on a cottage basis. It seems likely that in some regions many of them never became permanent chapels and eventually died out. In these cases they are now very difficult to track down, and since they are not necessarily recorded in the 1851 census they may well have been much more numerous than we now realize. Certainly they existed in a number of parishes in Shropshire where there is often no further evidence of organized Dissent.[1] They were particularly characteristic of sects like the Plymouth Brethren, whose numbers for this reason may have been considerably underestimated in the census.

The desire for the close fellowship of the chapel circle was also reflected in the antagonism of many early nineteenth-century religious groups to the conception of the church as a mere physical building, a 'temple made with hands', and their preoccupation with it instead as a community of people, a family of brothers and sisters. This antagonism must not be exaggerated, for in many cases the sacrifices of money, time, and materials made by humble people to build an edifice worthy to symbolize the permanence and prestige of their connexion in the local community were remarkable. Yet the buildings themselves

---

[1] Several are referred to in V.C.H., *Shropshire*, VIII (1968), covering the area south and west of Shrewsbury. In some areas many of them are recorded in the 1851 census.

were an outward and visible sign of something more profound: the formation of a body of men and women who felt themselves, in the Pauline phrase, to be members one of another, or in Petrine language 'built together' as living stones of the temple. This preoccupation with the church as a family was especially marked amongst bodies like the Brethren, who adopted their name specifically to distinguish themselves in this respect; but it was not confined to the Plymouth Brethren. They were simply a more extreme manifestation of a widespread movement of sensibility in Nonconformist circles generally. Religious groups like these in fact met a certain unsatisfied need of the time, the longing for a deeper personal communion of human soul with soul. At another level this movement linked with the concern of writers like George Eliot and Margaret Oliphant – both of whom, it is significant to note, spent much of their youth amongst Nonconformist groups of this kind – with the local community as a body of people, as a social organism. In this respect George Eliot and Mrs Oliphant contrast strikingly with later provincial authors, like Thomas Hardy and Mary Webb – unaware of Nonconformist experience or antagonistic to its basic conceptions – who were more preoccupied with the merely visual and atmospheric aspects of local society.

To the present writer a certain haunting sense of loneliness seems to have been a widespread phenomenon in early nineteenth-century society. "Here in the sea of life enisled", wrote Matthew Arnold, "we mortal millions live alone." At a very different level of experience from Arnold's, the innumerable chapels and cottage meetings of the time provided a kind of answer to this feeling of individual isolation. It was their emphasis on the church as a home, a family, a circle of affection, that lay behind the universal identification of 'home' with 'heaven' at this period. Nonconformity did not originate this identification; but it is interesting to note that it was one that was comparatively rarely met with in the sixteenth and early seventeenth centuries. The reference to heaven as the *home* of the exiled human spirit does not seem to become general in England till the time of the great Nonconformist Philip Doddridge in the 1730s and '40s. Several of Doddridge's writings, such as *The Family Expositor* (1739–56), in fact played a considerable part in the extraordinary idealization of domestic life during the late eighteenth and nineteenth centuries. To us the Victorian concern with the home circle and its sanctity may seem an obsession, and rather an insincere one; yet it would be a mistake not to sense behind the later sentimentality the hardly-won reality of earlier generations. Up to a point, after all, the reformation of domestic manners implicit in it was a civilizing influence in the rough and sometimes brutal family circumstances of the time.

Moreover, although the scope of the chapel community in a rural parish was necessarily small and its experience narrow, there were ways in which it could enlarge the capacities, deepen the feelings, and broaden the mind. "There is a sense", says Dr Leavis of *Adam Bede*, a novel in which Dissenting experience plays a large part, "in which, paradoxically, the inhabitants of that so provincial England live in a larger world than their successors."[1] In an enclosed community like the one George Eliot described people tend to look more to the past, to custom, to early attachments and impressions, than in a more open society. The past is the principal external avenue open to them, the past of their own local world, of their own 'connexion' and its families. Over the years the early experiences of the community come to be sublimated in its moral code and ideals, and loyalty to these becomes the supreme necessity, the absorbing interest, a claim superior to every external loyalty. And woven into the fabric of the Dissenting 'connexion' there was usually a nexus of local dynasties, whose history and relationships were inextricably bound up with its own story and gradually came to form a focus of interest and loyalty in themselves.[2]

Quite as important in enlarging the mental and emotional capacities of English men and women was that exploration of the inner world of mind and spirit which the New Dissent opened up for thousands of ordinary people. In these respects it is scarcely too much to claim that Nonconformity helped to reorient the mind of a nation. Its introspective powers and its preoccupation with family life go far to explain the concern with domestic sensibility and psychological development which was so characteristic a feature of Victorian novelists. Behind the development of the psychological novel one must envisage a long tradition of religious studies of human feeling, such as John Newton's widely read volume of letters, *Cardiphonia: or, the Utterance of the Heart* (1781). With their early Nonconformist connexions novelists like Mrs Gaskell, Margaret Oliphant, and George Eliot were profoundly influenced by this emphasis on religious introspection. True, the two latter authors subsequently rejected the theological assumptions behind it; yet it went far to shape their cast of thought, to extend their emotional range, and to stimulate their powers of psychological penetration. At the beginnings of psychology itself, it is interesting to find once again the figure of Philip Doddridge, who in the 1730s introduced the subject into his academy at Northampton under the name of 'pneumatology'.

Perhaps the most important factor of all in this extension of the limits of sensibility was the vast development of Dissenting hymnology at this time, beginning with Isaac Watts and Philip Doddridge and continuing through Charles Wesley and his many imitators well into the nineteenth century. One

[1] George Eliot, *Adam Bede*, Signet edn (1961), Foreword by F. R. Leavis, xiii.
[2] This is well brought out in several Victorian novels, for example in Margaret Oliphant's *Salem Chapel* (1863), and *Phoebe, Junior* (1876).

has only to read a single verse of one of Wesley's great hymns to realize that one has entered a different emotional world from that of the Puritanism of Stuart England. No Puritan could have written such lines as these:

> O Love Divine how sweet thou art,
> When shall I find my willing heart
> All taken up with thee?

For thousands of English people hymns like these opened up a range of thought and feeling far beyond the conception of their Protestant forebears.[1]

It was often for reasons such as these – the deepening of emotional and mental experience, the reformation of family life, the intensification of human fellowship and brotherhood – that so many millions of English people were prepared in the eighteenth and nineteenth centuries to cut themselves off from the established church and set up their own little religious commonwealths in the countless Zions and Bethels of the countryside. It has often been one of the complaints levelled against English Nonconformity that, by alienating itself from the established religious order, it broke down the unity of the country parish and destroyed the sense of local community. One does not need to believe in any golden age of rural life to admit a certain justice in these strictures.[2] Yet there is, after all, something to be said against too powerful a sense of local community. It can be intolerant, it can be cruel, and it can become unbearably narrow-minded. For Christians there is doubtless much to be ashamed of in quarrels and divisions. Yet one does not need any extensive acquaintance with ecclesiastical history, or much observation of developments in the contemporary religious world, to realize that there are also dangers in the plea for unity. All too often it has been advanced merely as an excuse for the persecution of minorities, sometimes as a cover for the unscrupulous designs of a doctrinaire pressure group. Where depth of feeling is involved, or integrity and independence of judgment are called for, there may be occasions, the old Dissenters thought, when it is best to part.

---

[1] Professor A. R. Humphreys makes some interesting remarks in this connexion in his article, 'Literature and Religion in Eighteenth-Century England', *Journal of Ecclesiastical History*, III (1952), 183–4.

[2] The disadvantages could often be real enough. In Hasted's day nearly half the population of Maidstone were said to be Nonconformists, chiefly Presbyterians and Baptists, and the "dissension in matters of religion unhappily extends in politics, and from the heat of parties, destroys much of that social intercourse and harmony which would otherwise unite the inhabitants of this flourishing town." Hasted, *op. cit.*, IV, 263.

APPENDIX

Table I Distribution of Dissent in Kent in 1676[1]

	Parishes	Conformists No.	Conformists %	Non-conformists No.	Non-conformists %	Papists No.	Total No.
A RURAL PARISHES							
I *East Kent*							
North-East Marshlands	18	1,347	98	20	2	—	1,367
Foothills	41	4,639	93	338	7	7	4,984
Downland	42	5,222	97	179	3	2	5,403
Forest of Blean	8	1,165	94	68	6	8	1,241
Romney Marsh	22	1,016	92	82[2]	8	—	1,098
Total	131	13,389	95	687	5	17	14,093
II *Mid-Kent*							
Foothills	20	2,418	99	8	0.3	26	2,452
Downland	18	1,927	98	24	1	6	1,957
Chartland	33	5,107	95	255	5	9	5,371
Weald	33	9,667	83	1,986	17	29	11,682
Total	104	19,119	89	2,273	11	70	21,462
III *West Kent*							
Thames-side parishes and Hoo	11	1,066	99	16	1	—	1,082
Foothills	12	2,087	98	34	2	3	2,124
Downland	16	1,529	99	19	1	1	1,549
Chartland	17	2,052	97	52[3]	3	11	2,115
Weald	16	5,483	96	177	4	27	5,687
Total	72	12,217	97	298	3	42	12,557
IV *Unclassifiable Rural Parishes*	9	1,402	82	315	8	1	1,718
V *All Rural Parishes*	316	46,127	93	3,573	7	130	49,830
B URBAN PARISHES	34	17,535	83	3,464	17	63	21,062
C ALL PARISHES	350	63,662	90	7,037	10	193	70,892

NOTES:

[1] The Compton Census, on which the figures are based, does not cover the whole of Kent. There are no surviving returns for 53 parishes, of which the chief group is the 31 parishes of the deanery of Shoreham in west Kent. The 350 parishes covered by the surviving returns therefore represent about seven-eighths of the county.

[2] Of these, 50 were in Lydd parish.   [3] Of these, 40 were in Snodland parish.

Table II   General Religious Allegiance in 1851

		Total Church and Chapel Sittings	Anglicans Sittings	%	Dissenters Sittings	%	
1.	Herefordshire	68,675	49,312	72	19,363	28	41
2.	Rutland	17,299	12,131	70	5,168	30	40
3.	Oxfordshire	109,301	74,369	68	34,932	32	39
4.	Sussex	160,011	108,076	67	51,935	33	38
5.	Surrey	219,094	143,783	66	75,311	34	37
6.	Westmorland[1]	37,239	24,411	66	12,828	34	36
7.	Dorset	120,082	77,886	65	42,196	35	35
8.	Kent	299,296	194,443	65	104,853	35	34
9.	Hampshire	212,161	135,720	64	76,441	36	33
10.	Shropshire	143,663	92,435	64	51,228	36	32
11.	Suffolk[2]	224,229	141,417	63	82,812	37	31
12.	Middlesex	552,231	344,487	62	207,744	38	30
13.	Berkshire	92,737	56,679	61	36,058	39	29
14.	Essex	216,113	132,041	61	84,072	39	28
15.	Somerset	287,353	174,723	61	112,630	39	27
16.	Warwickshire	201,831	123,624	61	78,207	39	26
17.	Worcestershire	138,668	85,155	61	53,513	39	25
18.	Norfolk[2]	283,420	168,722	60	114,698	40	24
19.	Hertfordshire	93,230	55,193	59	38,037	41	23
20.	Devon	332,934	191,710	58	141,224	42	22
21.	Staffordshire	279,516	161,217	58	118,299	42	21
22.	Buckinghamshire	113,209	64,231	57	48,978	43	20
23.	Cumberland	99,783	56,803	57	42,980	43	19
24.	Gloucestershire	276,606	156,651	57	119,955	43	18
25.	Northamptonshire	150,472	84,816	56	65,656	44	17
26.	Wiltshire	158,694	87,843	55	70,851	45	16
27.	Lancashire	708,217	383,466	54	324,751	46	15
28.	Cheshire	229,711	121,882	53	107,829	47	14
29.	Leicestershire	156,678	82,964	53	73,714	47	13
30.	Huntingdonshire	45,014	23,568	52	21,446	48	12
31.	Cambridgeshire	104,196	52,917	51	51,279	49	11
32.	Lincolnshire	279,247	142,844	51	136,403	49	10
33.	North Riding	161,062	79,740	50	81,322	50	9
34.	Bedfordshire	87,814	42,557	48	45,257	52	8
35.	Derbyshire	182,581	87,829	48	94,752	52	7
36.	Nottinghamshire	150,024	70,928	47	79,096	53	6
37.	East Riding	140,793	64,135	46	76,658	54	5
38.	West Riding	665,428	276,910	42	388,518	58	4
39.	Co. Durham	167,285	66,319	40	100,966	60	3
40.	Northumberland	131,646	52,405	40	79,241	60	2
41.	Cornwall	261,684	95,155	36	166,529	64	1
	Total	8,359,227	4,641,497	56	3,717,730	44	

NOTES:

[1] The number of sittings in the four Baptist chapels in the county was not reported. These have been estimated at 1,000.

[2] The figures for Anglican sittings in these counties particularly are probably affected by the exceptional size and number of ancient parish churches.

Table III   Landholding and Rural Dissent in Four Counties, c. 1860: A
(Figures in Percentages)[1]

Type of Parish	(a) No Chapel	(b) One Chapel	(c) Two Chapels	(d) Three or More Chapels	Total of (b), (c), and (d)
I *Property in One Hand*					
Kent	—	—	—	—	—
Lindsey	97	1.5	—	1.5	3
Leicestershire	100	—	—	—	—
Northamptonshire	97	3	—	—	3
II *Property in a Few Hands*					
Kent	86	10	3	1	14
Lindsey	74	16	8	2	26
Leicestershire	68	25	6	1	32
Northamptonshire	71	21	7	1	29
Total of I and II					
Kent	86	10	3	1	14
Lindsey	82	11	5	2	18
Leicestershire	73	21	5	1	27
Northamptonshire	75	18	6	1	25
III *Property Subdivided*					
Kent	52	46	2	—	48
Lindsey	12	35	41	12	88
Leicestershire	18	50	20	12	82
Northamptonshire	22	40	31	7	78
IV *Property Much Subdivided*					
Kent	17	56	19	8	83
Lindsey	15	19	36	30	85
Leicestershire	15	28	16	41	85
Northamptonshire	24	29	31	16	76
Total of III and IV					
Kent	30	53	12	5	70
Lindsey	14	25	38	23	86
Leicestershire	17	39	18	26	83
Northamptonshire	23	35	31	11	77
All Types of Parish					
Kent	61	29	7	3	39
Lindsey	53	17	19	11	47
Leicestershire	45	30	12	13	55
Northamptonshire	58	24	14	4	42

NOTE:

[1] In the cases of Lindsey and Leicestershire the percentages include 'probable' as well as 'certain' parishes. The former comprise 37 per cent of the total of 374 in Lindsey and 26 per cent of the total of 250 in Leicestershire. In Kent and Northamptonshire the 'probable' percentage is negligible (out of 340 and 282 parishes respectively). For 30 parishes in Kent, 33 in Lindsey, 20 in Leicestershire, and 28 in Northamptonshire, information is inadequate, and these have been excluded from the table.

Table IV   Landholding and Rural Dissent in Four Counties, c. 1860: B
(Figures in Percentages)[1]

Type of Parish	(a) Property in One Hand	(b) Property in a Few Hands	(c) Total of (a) and (b)	Property Sub-divided	(d) Property Much Sub-divided	Total of (c) and (d)
I No Chapel						
Kent	—	78	78	14	8	22
Lindsey	35	54	89	3	8	11
Leicestershire	17	65	82	10	8	18
Northamptonshire	17	70	87	7	6	13
II One Chapel						
Kent	—	19	19	25	56	81
Lindsey	2	37	39	31	30	61
Leicestershire	—	36	36	41	23	64
Northamptonshire	2	50	52	32	16	48
III Two Chapels						
Kent	—	21	21	4	75	79
Lindsey	—	17	17	33	50	83
Leicestershire	—	24	24	41	35	76
Northamptonshire	—	27	27	43	30	73
IV Three or More Chapels						
Kent	—	11	11	—	89	89
Lindsey	2	7	9	18	73	91
Leicestershire	—	3	3	21	76	97
Northamptonshire	—	9	9	36	55	91
Total of II, III, and IV						
Kent	—	19	19	20	61	81
Lindsey	1	22	23	29	48	77
Leicestershire	—	26	26	36	38	74
Northamptonshire	1	39	40	36	24	60
Total of III and IV						
Kent	—	18	18	3	79	82
Lindsey	1	14	15	27	58	85
Leicestershire	—	13	13	31	56	87
Northamptonshire	—	24	24	41	35	76
All Types of Parish						
Kent	—	55	55[2]	16[2]	29[2]	45[2]
Lindsey	20	39	59	15	26	41
Leicestershire	8	44	52	24	24	48
Northamptonshire	10	57	67	20	13	33

NOTES:
[1] In the cases of Lindsey and Leicestershire the percentages include 'probable' as well as 'certain' parishes. The former comprise 37 per cent of the total of 374 in Lindsey and 26 per cent of the total of 250 in Leicestershire. In Kent and Northamptonshire the 'probable' percentage is negligible (out of

340 and 282 parishes respectively). For 30 parishes in Kent, 33 in Lindsey, 20 in Leicestershire, and 28 in Northamptonshire information is inadequate, and these have been excluded from the table.

² These percentages, based on the number of parishes, distort the situation in Kent, where parish sizes varied much more widely than in the three other counties. The average 'estate' parish in Kent covered only 1,811 acres, compared with 3,514 acres for the average 'subdivided' parish and 4,253 acres for the average parish where land was 'much subdivided'. In terms of *acreage* the figures for Kent are as follows:

Property in a Few Hands: 340,460 acres=36 per cent of total area covered by the table
Property Subdivided: 189,766 acres=20 per cent of total area covered by the table
Property Much Subdivided: 416,809 acres=44 per cent of total area covered by the table

The 'freeholders' parishes' in Kent thus covered 64 per cent of the total area, and the 'estate parishes' 36 per cent. The latter figure compares with 52 per cent in Leicestershire, 59 per cent in Lindsey, and 67 per cent in Northamptonshire, based on the number of parishes in these three counties. Probably 'freeholders' parishes' in these three counties were also somewhat larger than 'estate parishes', but the disparity was relatively slight compared with Kent.

Table V   Industrial Villages in Leicestershire and Northamptonshire:
Number of Chapels

(L=Leicestershire; N=Northamptonshire; T=Total)

	Villages			Total Chapels		
	L	N	T	L	N	T
No chapel	7	7	14	0	0	0
One chapel	19	16	35	19	16	35
Two chapels	16	12	28	32	24	56
Three chapels	10	4	14	30	12	42
Four chapels	8	3	11	32	12	44
Five chapels	1	0	1	5	0	5
Total	61[1]	42[2]	103	118	64	182

NOTES:
[1] At least 11 of these had formerly been market centres, and probably six others.
[2] At least 14 of these had formerly been market centres, and probably four others.

Table VI   Industrial Villages in Leicestershire and Northamptonshire:
Types of Chapel

	Leicestershire	Northamptonshire	Total
Independents	14	8	22
Baptists	25	19	44
Wesleyans	29	14	43
Primitive Methodists	13	4	17
Quakers	0	1	1
Unspecified	37	18	55
Total	118	64	182

Table VII Industrial Villages in Leicestershire and Northamptonshire:
Types of Industry

	Leicestershire Villages	Northamptonshire Villages	Total
Framework-knitting	45	I	46
Shoemaking	0	16	16
Quarrying	6	10	16
Lacemaking	2	12	14
Coalmining	7	0	7
Brick- and tile-making	4	I	5
Malting and brewing	3	I	4
Iron-ore working	I	3	4
Iron-working	I	3	4
Lime-burning	2	I	3
Silkweaving	I	2	3
Water traffic	I	2	3
Glovemaking	2	0	2
Matmaking	I	2	3
Leather factories	0	2	2
Other industries	7[1]	5[2]	12
Total (Villages)[3]	61	42	103
Total (Industries)	20	18	28

NOTES:

  [1] One instance of each of the following: embroidery, earthenware manufacture, smallware-making, basket-making, boiler-making, needle-making, gypsum working.

  [2] One instance of each of the following: whipmaking, red ochre working, rush collar making, turnery, peppermint-oil distilling.

  [3] In some villages more than one industry was carried on, so that the totals in this line do not represent totals of figures in the column above.

Table VIII Leicestershire and Northamptonshire: Industrial Village Chapels

Framework-Knitting		Shoemaking		Lacemaking		Quarrying	
Villages	Chapels	Villages	Chapels	Villages	Chapels	Villages	Chapels
46	94	16	32	14	26	16	23

Table IX   Occupations in 17 Midland Parishes, 1777–98[1]
(Percentages)

	Spratton	Moulton	Harding-stone	Kings-thorpe	Hanslope	Raven-stone	Ten Agri-cultural Parishes[2]	Stoke Golding-ton	Compari-son with Northamp-ton Borough
1. Gentry	3	1	3	1	0	0	1	0	2
2. Professions	0	0	0	0	1	2	0	0	3
3. Wayfaring, Innkeeping, etc.	1	3	2	0	2	2	1	0	7
4. Processing and Wholesale Trades	15 ⎱60	4 ⎱43	3 ⎱40	9 ⎱33	2 ⎱33	2 ⎱28	6 ⎱24	0 ⎱7	8 ⎱78[5]
5. Retail Trades	11 ⎰	6 ⎰	0 ⎰	4 ⎰	9 ⎰	9 ⎰	2 ⎰	1 ⎰	10 ⎰
6. Crafts	33	30	35	20	19	13	15	6	50
7. Landwork[3]	20	14	6	13	10	9	14	10	3
8. Servants and Labourers[4]	18	41	51	52	57	62	61	83	18
Dissenting Chapels, 1851[6]	I, B	B, 2W	—	B	B, W	—	I, B, 2W[7]	I	17[8]

NOTES:

[1] All these parishes are in west Northamptonshire, except Hanslope, Ravenstone, and Stoke Goldington, which are on the Northamptonshire border of Buckinghamshire. The figures are based on the Northamptonshire Militia List of 1777 (Northants. County Record Office) and the Buckinghamshire *Posse Comitatus* of 1798 (Bucks. County Record Office).

[2] Abington, Great and Little Billing, Boughton, Overstone, Pitsford, Weston Favell, Dallington, Duston, Upton.

[3] Farmers, gardeners, graziers, and yeomen only. 'Yeoman' and 'farmer' seem to be synonymous terms in these villages: one term is used in one place, the other in another. The word 'husbandman' never occurs. 'Yeoman' does not appear in Buckinghamshire.

[4] Perhaps between two-thirds and three-quarters of these may have been agricultural workers, except in Northampton borough. Northampton labourers and servants often seem to be listed with their masters, none of whom were 'farmers', and very few 'gardeners' or 'yeomen'.

[5] No doubt most of the 'servants' and 'labourers' in Northampton worked for masters in these categories, so that the total percentage engaged under these heads in the borough was probably at least 90 per cent.

[6] I = Independents, B = Baptists, W = Wesleyans.

[7] The Independent and Baptist chapels, both in Duston parish, were probably at St James's End, which was in fact a suburb of Northampton by 1861.

[8] Independents (3), Baptists (5), Quakers, Unitarians, Wesleyans (3), Primitive Methodists, Latter-day Saints, Swedenborgians, and an 'isolated congregation'. Dissenters outnumbered Anglicans in Northampton.

Table X Religious Allegiance in Four Counties in 1851

	Acreage	Population in 1861	Parishes	Anglicans		Independents		Baptists		Wesleyan Methodists		Primitive Methodists		Other Methodists		Other Dissenters[1]		All Dissenters	
				C	S	C	S	C	S	C	S	C	S	C	S	C	S	C	S
Kent	1,013,838	733,887	425	479	194,443 65%	86	27,091 9%	107	25,668 8%	184	33,759 11%	26	2,877	45	7,285	52	8,173 3%	500	104,853 35%
										\} 255(C); 43,921(S) 15%									
Leicestershire	514,164	237,412	214	289	82,964 53%	41	11,988 8%	85	24,001 15%	129	21,739 14%	53	7,930	20	3,523	26	4,533 3%	354	73,714 47%
										\} 202(C); 33,192(S) 21%									
Lincolnshire[2]	1,775,457	412,246	621	657	142,844 51%	38	11,508 4%	62	13,620 5%	462	78,862 28%	221	25,164	21	4,517	27	2,732 1%	831	136,403 49%
										\} 704(C); 108,543(S) 39%									
Northamptonshire	630,358	231,079	303	292	84,816 56%	56	17,444 12%	87	23,200 16%	97	18,620 12%	16	1,759	9	992	29	3,641 2%	294	65,656 44%
										\} 122(C); 21,371(S) 14%									

75

NOTES:

C = churches or chapels   S = number of sittings

[1] Excluding Roman Catholics and Jews.

[2] The figures for Lindsey are not given separately, except in the case of acreage (996,604) and population (229,816).

Table XI   Landholding in Four Counties, *1860*

	Total	(a) In One Hand	(b) In a Few Hands	Total (a) and (b)	(c) Sub-divided	(d) Much Sub-divided	Total (c) and (d)
Kent[1]							
Parishes	340	—	188	188	54	98	152
Percentage	100	—	55	55	16	29	45
Lindsey							
Parishes	374	73	146	219	57	98	155
Percentage	100	20	39	59	15	26	41
Leicestershire							
Parishes	250	20	109	129	60	61	121
Percentage	100	8	44	52	24	24	48
Northamptonshire							
Parishes	282	29	160	189	55	38	93
Percentage	100	10	57	67	20	13	33

NOTE:

[1] The figures for Kent are misleading owing to the wide variation in size of parish in this county. See also Table XXIV, which shows that in terms of *acreage* 64 per cent of the county was 'subdivided' or 'much subdivided'.

Table XII   Lindsey: Landholding and Rural Dissent, c. 1860: A[1]

Type of Parish	No Chapel	One Chapel	Two Chapels	Three or More Chapels	Total
I *Property in One Hand*					
Parishes	71	1	—	1	73
Percentage	97	1.5	—	1.5	100
II *Property in a Few Hands*					
Parishes	107	24	12	3	146
Percentage	74	16	8	2	100
III *Property Subdivided*					
Parishes	7	20	23	7	57
Percentage	12	35	41	12	100
IV *Property Much Subdivided*					
Parishes	15	19	35	29	98
Percentage	15	19	36	30	100
Total of I and II					
Parishes	178	25	12	4	219
Percentage	81	11	5	2	100
Total of III and IV					
Parishes	22	39	58	36	155
Percentage	14	25	38	23	100
All Parishes	200	64	70	40	374
Percentage	53	17	19	11	100

NOTE:

[1] The figures include 'probable' as well as 'certain' parishes. These comprise 37 per cent of the total of 374.

Table XIII   Lindsey: Landholding and Rural Dissent, c. 1860: B[1]

Type of Parish	Property in One Hand	Property in a Few Hands	Property Sub-divided	Property Much Sub-divided	All Parishes
I *No Chapel*					
Parishes	71	107	7	15	200
Percentage	35	54	3	8	100
II *One Chapel*					
Parishes	1	24	20	19	64
Percentage	2	38	31	30	100
III *Two Chapels*					
Parishes	—	12	23	35	70
Percentage	—	17	33	50	100
IV *Three or More Chapels*					
Parishes	1	3	7	29	40
Percentage	2	7	18	73	100
Total of II, III, and IV					
Parishes	2	39	50	83	174
Percentage	1	22	29	48	100
Total of III and IV					
Parishes	1	15	30	64	110
Percentage	1	14	27	58	100
All Parishes	73	146	57	98	374
Percentage	20	39	15	26	100

NOTE:

[1] The figures include 'probable' as well as 'certain' parishes. These comprise 37 per cent of the total of 374.

Table XIV   Leicestershire: Landholding and Rural Dissent, c. 1860: A[1]

Type of Parish	No Chapel	One Chapel	Two Chapels	Three or More Chapels	Total
I *Property in One Hand*					
Parishes	20	—	—	—	20
Percentage	100	—	—	—	100
II *Property in a Few Hands*					
Parishes	74	27	7	1	109
Percentage	68	25	6	1	100
III *Property Subdivided*					
Parishes	11	30	12	7	60
Percentage	18	50	20	12	100
IV *Property Much Subdivided*					
Parishes	9	17	10	25	61
Percentage	15	28	16	41	100
Total of I and II					
Parishes	94	27	7	1	129
Percentage	73	21	5	1	100
Total of III and IV					
Parishes	20	47	22	32	121
Percentage	17	39	18	26	100
All Parishes	114	74	29	33	250
Percentage	45	30	12	13	100

NOTE:

[1] The figures include 'probable' as well as 'certain' parishes. These comprise 26 per cent of the total of 250.

Table XV Leicestershire: Landholding and Rural Dissent, c. 1860: B[1]

Type of Parish	Property in One Hand	Property in a Few Hands	Property Sub-divided	Property Much Sub-divided	All Parishes
I *No Chapel*					
Parishes	20	74	11	9	114
Percentage	17	65	10	8	100
II *One Chapel*					
Parishes	—	27	30	17	74
Percentage	—	36	41	23	100
III *Two Chapels*					
Parishes	—	7	12	10	29
Percentage	—	24	41	35	100
IV *Three or More Chapels*					
Parishes	—	1	7	25	33
Percentage	—	3	21	76	100
Total of II, III, and IV					
Parishes	—	35	49	52	136
Percentage	—	26	36	38	100
Total of III and IV					
Parishes	—	8	19	35	62
Percentage	—	13	31	56	100
All Parishes	20	109	60	61	250
Percentage	8	44	24	24	100

NOTE:

[1] The figures include 'probable' as well as 'certain' parishes. These comprise 26 per cent of the total of 250.

Table XVI   Northamptonshire: Landholding and Rural Dissent, c. 1860: A

Type of Parish	No Chapel	One Chapel	Two Chapels	Three or More Chapels	Total
I *Property in One Hand*					
Parishes	28	1	—	—	29
Percentage	97	3	—	—	100
II *Property in a Few Hands*					
Parishes	114	34	11	1	160
Percentage	71	21	7	1	100
III *Property Subdivided*					
Parishes	12	22	17	4	55
Percentage	22	40	31	7	100
IV *Property Much Subdivided*					
Parishes	9	11	12	6	38
Percentage	24	29	31	16	100
Total of I and II					
Parishes	142	35	11	1	189
Percentage	75	18	6	1	100
Total of III and IV					
Parishes	21	33	29	10	93
Percentage	23	35	31	11	100
All Parishes	163	68	40	11	282
Percentage	58	24	14	4	100

Table XVII   Northamptonshire: Landholding and Rural Dissent, c. 1860: B

Type of Parish	Property in One Hand	Property in a Few Hands	Property Sub- divided	Property Much Sub- divided	All Parishes
I *No Chapel*					
Parishes	28	114	12	9	163
Percentage	17	70	7	6	100
II *One Chapel*					
Parishes	1	34	22	11	68
Percentage	2	50	32	16	100
III *Two Chapels*					
Parishes	—	11	17	12	40
Percentage	—	27	43	30	100
IV *Three or More Chapels*					
Parishes	—	1	4	6	11
Percentage	—	9	36	55	100
Total of II, III, and IV					
Parishes	1	46	43	29	119
Percentage	1	39	36	24	100
Total of III and IV					
Parishes	—	12	21	18	51
Percentage	—	24	41	35	100
All Parishes	29	160	55	38	282
Percentage	10	57	20	13	100

Table XVIII   Church and Chapel Sittings in 1851

	Kent	Leicester-shire	Lincoln-shire	Northampton-shire
I *Population*	733,887	237,412	412,246	231,079
II *Church/Chapel Sittings*	299,296	156,678	279,247	150,472
III *II as % of I*	41	66	68	65
IV *Anglicans (%)*	65	53	51	56
V *Dissenters (%)*	35	47	49	44
(a) Independents	9 ⎫ 17	8 ⎫ 23	4 ⎫ 9	12 ⎫ 28
(b) Baptists	8 ⎭	15 ⎭	5 ⎭	16 ⎭
(c) Methodists	15	21	39	14
i. Wesleyans	11	14	28	12
ii. Others[1]	4	7	11	2
(d) Other Dissenters	3	3	1	2

NOTE:

[1] Principally Primitive Methodists, except in Kent, where the Bible Christians were the most numerous branch of Methodism apart from Wesleyans.

Table XIX   Churches and Chapels in 1851

	Kent	Leicester-shire	Lincoln-shire	Northampton-shire
I *Acreage*	1,013,838	514,164	1,775,457	630,358
II *Parishes*	425	214	621	303
III *Anglican Churches*	479	289	657	292
IV *Dissenting Chapels*	500	354	831	294
(a) Independents	86	41	38	56
(b) Baptists	107	85	62	87
(c) Methodists	255	202	704	122
i. Wesleyans	184	129	462	97
ii. Others	71	73	242	25
(d) Other Dissenters	52	26	27	29
V *All Churches and Chapels*	979	643	1,488	586
VI *Inhabitants per Church and Chapel*	750	369	277	394
VII *Inhabitants per Chapel*	1,468	671	496	786

Table XX   The Population of Five Counties, 1801–61

	1801	1861	Increase
Kent	308,667	733,887	138%
Leicestershire	130,082	237,412	83%
Lincolnshire	208,624	412,246	98%
Northamptonshire	131,525	227,704	73%
Staffordshire	242,693	746,943	207%
England and Wales	8,892,536	20,066,224	126%

Table XXI   Rural Dissent in Kent in 1851: Regional Analysis

District[1]	Parishes (Total= 261)	Anglicans			Dissenters		
		Churches	Sittings Nos.	%	Chapels	Sittings Nos.	%
Bridge	23	23	5,059	85	10	890	15
Blean	13	14	6,324	80	12	1,624	20
East Ashford	25	21	3,911	79	9	1,042	21
Romney Marsh	19	13	3,371	78	7	975	22
Hollingbourne	23	23	5,487	72	15	2,157	28
Hoo	7	7	1,266	72	5	505	28
West Ashford	13	13	7,146	70	15	3,028	30
Elham	20	21	7,075	67	21	3,562	33
Faversham	24	25	6,658	67	22	3,285	33
Sevenoaks	15	21	6,987	65	28	3,844	35
Tonbridge	11	16	9,420	65	22	5,208	35
Cranbrook	6	8	4,752	64	17	2,685	36
Tenterden	11	12	4,762	64	17	2,650	36
Maidstone	15	21	10,845	62	42	6,743	38
Medway	5	15	9,639	60	24	6,492	40
Canterbury	17[2]	13	4,886	60	8	3,320	40
Thanet	10	13	12,333	56	33	9,485	44
Greenwich	4	16	16,907	54	43	14,311	46

NOTES:

[1] These districts together comprised nearly two-thirds of the county. A number of them were co-terminous with the old subdivisions of the lathes and still exist as local government areas. The modern rural district of Sevenoaks, for example, corresponds to the old lathal subdivision of Sutton-at-Hone Nether.

[2] All in the city of Canterbury. Several of these parishes had, by 1851, lost their churches and been amalgamated with those adjacent.

Table XXII   Rural and Urban Chapels in Four Counties in 1851

		All Chapels	Rural Chapels[1]	Urban Chapels[1]
Kent:	Numbers	500	178	322
	Percentage	100	36	64
Leicestershire:	Numbers	354	245	109
	Percentage	100	69	31
Lindsey:	Numbers	547[2]	344[2]	203[2]
	Percentage	100	63	37
Northamptonshire:	Numbers	294	187	107
	Percentage	100	64	36

NOTES:

[1] Probably these figures in each case slightly underestimate the proportion of rural chapels and over-estimate urban chapels, because rural parishes for which information seemed inadequate or unreliable have been excluded for purposes of this study (cf. p. 70, n. 1). It is unlikely, however, that any adjustment would affect the figures by more than 2 or 3 per cent.

[2] The figure for Lindsey is not given separately. This is the total for the seven Lindsey registration districts (Lincoln, Horncastle, Spilsby, Louth, Caistor, Glanford Brigg, Gainsborough). In some cases the boundaries of these districts overlapped with adjacent areas, so that the above total is approximate only.

Table XXIII   Kent: Dissent in the Most Strongly Anglican Areas in 1851
(Number of Sittings)

District	Parishes	Methodists	Congregationalists	Baptists	Others
Romney Marsh	19	741	—	234	—
Blean	13	837	757	—	30
Bridge	23	730	160	—	—
East Ashford	25	839	—	203	—
Hollingbourne	23	879	1,038	240	—
Hoo	7	265	—	120	120
West Ashford	13	1,451	—	1,395	180
Elham	20	1,730	620	643	425
Faversham	24	2,134	751	300	100
Total	167	9,606	3,326	3,135	855
		=57%	7,316=43%		
Percentage for whole county		42%	58%		

Table XXIV   *Distribution of Property in Kent, 1860: A*[1]

	Number of Parishes	Acreage	Average Parish Acreage	Percentage of total Acreage
Property in a Few Hands	188	340,460	1,811	36
Property Subdivided	54	189,766	3,514	20
Property Much Subdivided	98	416,809	4,253	44
Total	340	947,035	2,785	100

NOTE:

[1] Urban parishes have been excluded. In many cases (e.g., Tonbridge and Maidstone) these included considerable tracts of countryside, but it has proved impossible to distinguish between their urban and rural parts in terms of acreage and landownership. These urban parishes amounted in all to about 65,000 acres.

Table XXV   Distribution of Property in Kent, 1860: B

	Parishes in a Few Hands	Parishes Sub-divided	Parishes Much Sub-divided	Total
A *Weald and Forest*				
Western	5	3	9	17
Mid Kent	2	—	10	12
Southern	1	4	5	10
Blean	1	3	4	8
Total	9 (19%)	10 (21%)	28 (60%)	47
B *Chartland*				
Holmesdale	10	3	8	21
Mid Kent	18	8	8	34
Eastern Weald and Chartland	19	5	8	32
Total	47 (54%)	16 (18%)	24 (28%)	87
C *Downland*				
Western	14	9	4	27
Mid Kent	11	2	2	15
Eastern	34	3	5	42
Total	59 (70%)	14 (17%)	11 (13%)	84
D *Foothills*				
Western	9	2	5	16
Mid Kent	17	7	6	30
Stour valleys	25	5	11	41
Thanet	4	—	—	4
Total	55 (61%)	14 (15%)	22 (24%)	91
E *Other Areas*				
Thames-side	1	—	2	3
Hoo, Sheppey, and Swale	17	2	—	19
Romney Marsh	9	1	7	17
Total[1]	197 (57%)	57 (16%)	94 (27%)	348

NOTES:

The percentages are more significant than the absolute figures because of the wide variation in average parish size between each region.

[1] The percentages in this line are not of great significance because of the wide disparity in size of parishes as between Wealden, Chartland, Downland, and Foothill areas. The total differs by eight from the total (340) in the analysis of chapels (Table XXVII), because for a few parishes there is information on landholding but not on chapels.

Table XXVI   Distribution of Property in Kent, 1860: C[1]

	Parishes in a Few Hands	Parishes Sub-divided	Parishes Much Sub-divided	Total
A *West Kent*				
Weald	5	3	9	17
Holmesdale	10	3	8	21
Downland	14	9	4	27
Foothills	9	2	5	16
Thames-side	1	—	2	3
Total	39 (46%)	17 (21%)	28 (33%)	84
B *Mid Kent*				
Weald	2	—	10	12
Chartland	18	8	8	34
Downland	11	2	2	15
Foothills	17	7	6	30
Hoo, Sheppey, and Swale	17	2	0	19
Total	65 (59%)	19 (17%)	26 (24%)	110
C *East Kent*				
Southern Weald	1	4	5	10
Eastern Weald and Chartland	19	5	8	32
Downland	34	3	5	42
Stour valleys	25	5	11	41
Total	79 (63%)	17 (14%)	29 (23%)	125
D *Other Regions*				
Forest of Blean	1	3	4	8
Isle of Thanet	4	—	—	4
Romney Marsh	9	1	7	17
Total	14	4	11	29
Total	197 (57%)	57 (16%)	94 (27%)	348[2]

NOTES:

[1] In interpreting the figures in the table, it should be remembered that they refer to the *number of parishes* and not to the *acreage of land*: in terms of acreage the picture would be very different from that given above, since the average parish where land was in a few hands covered only 1,811 acres, whereas subdivided parishes covered 3,514 acres on average, and much subdivided parishes 4,253 acres. In terms of acreage the subdivided and much subdivided parishes covered 64 per cent of the county, though only 43 per cent of the 348 parishes in the table.

[2] The total differs by eight from the total (340) in the analysis of chapels (Table XXVII), because for a few parishes there is information on landholding but not on chapels.

Table XXVII   Kent: Landholding and Rural Dissent, c. 1860: A[1]

Type of Parish	No Chapel	One Chapel	Two Chapels	Three or More Chapels	Total
I *Property in a Few Hands*					
Parishes	163	19	5	1	188
Percentage	86	10	3	1	100
II *Property Subdivided*					
Parishes	28	25	1	—	54
Percentage	52	46	2	—	100
III *Property Much Subdivided*					
Parishes	17[2]	55	18	8	98
Percentage	17	57	18	8	100
Total of II and III					
Parishes	45	80	19	8	152
Percentage	30	53	12	5	100
All Parishes	208	99	24	9	340
Percentage	61	29	7	3	100

NOTES:

[1] In this county there was apparently not a single parish in which all the property was in one hand.

[2] Ten of these 17 parishes consisted largely of marshland divided amongst many non-resident owners, but with few resident proprietors.

Table XXVIII   Kent: Landholding and Rural Dissent, c. 1860: B[1]

Type of Parish	Property in a Few Hands	Property Subdivided	Property Much Subdivided	All Parishes
I *No Chapel*				
Parishes	163	28	17	208
Percentage	78	14	8	100
II *One Chapel*				
Parishes	19	25	55	99
Percentage	19	25	56	100
III *Two Chapels*				
Parishes	5	1	18	24
Percentage	21	4	75	100
IV *Three or More Chapels*				
Parishes	1	—	8	9
Percentage	11	—	89	100
Total of II, III, and IV				
Parishes	25	26	81	132
Percentage	19	20	61	100
Total of III and IV				
Parishes	6	1	26	33
Percentage	18	3	79	100
All Parishes	188	54	98	340
Percentage	55	16	29	100

NOTE:

[1] In this county there was apparently not a single parish in which all the property was in one hand.

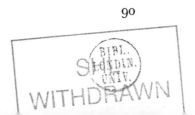
BIBL. S... DUBLIN. UNIV. WITHDRAWN